environmet 333.72.

GREEN GUIDES

NORTHBROOK COLLEGE SUSSEX
BW

Further, Higher and Adult Education

Library and Information Services

Littlehampton Road site	Tel: 01903 606213
Broadwater Road site	Tel: 01903 606451

This book must be returned to the library, or renewed, on or before the date last entered below.
Renewal can be granted only when the book has not been previously requested by another borrower.

-8 MAR 2011		
24 MAY 2011		
24 MAY 2011		
10 JUN 2011		
18/3/20		

D1494319

PLEASE PROTECT BOOKS FROM DAMAGE   D.9304

This is a **FLAME TREE** book
First published in 2009

Publisher and Creative Director: Nick Wells
Project Editor: Victoria Lyle
Art Director: Mike Spender
Layout Design: Dave Jones
Digital Design and Production: Chris Herbert
Picture Research: Victoria Lyle
Copy Editor: Polly Prior
Proofreader: Alexandra Davidson
Indexer: Helen Snaith

Special thanks to Rebecca Kidd, Polly Prior, Samantha Shore

09 11 13 12 10
1 3 5 7 9 10 8 6 4 2

This edition first published 2009 by
FLAME TREE PUBLISHING
Crabtree Hall, Crabtree Lane
Fulham, London SW6 6TY
United Kingdom

www.flametreepublishing.com

Flame Tree Publishing is part of The Foundry Creative Media Co. Ltd

ISBN 978-1-84786-530-4

Printed in India

GREEN GUIDES

Living Green

MARIA COSTANTINO

Foreword by **PENNEY POYZER**

**FLAME TREE
PUBLISHING**

Contents

Lots of ideas for reducing, reusing and recycling waste; from stopping junk mail to reupholstering tired furniture and passing on old magazines to your doctor's waiting room. Remember, there is a difference between what you want and what you need – recognizing this could help you start reducing your waste today. Our throwaway mentality means that we often put things in the bin instead of repairing them; this means that all sorts of junk ends up in landfill when it could be reused. And while many of us have got into the habit of recycling our cans and bottles, find out what other items, large and small, can also be recycled.

This chapter explains what a carbon footprint is and provides lots of information about how you can reduce yours in your home. Key to this is not wasting energy by turning things off when they are not in use. Keeping cold air out and warm air in with insulation and draught exclusion is also a good place to start. The great thing about reducing your energy consumption is that you

will save money too! Renewable energy sources, such as hydro, wind and solar power, and the advantages of each, are discussed, as is water and ways to conserve this precious resource.

All those chemicals in your cleaning products are not necessarily good for you or the environment. Luckily, nature has supplied some excellent alternatives that will get your home just as clean. Bicarbonate of soda and vinegar can be used in numerous ways in your kitchen, bathroom and laundry. Other greener cleaners include lemons, salt, hydrogen peroxide, eucalyptus oil and borax. From deodorizing carpets, to removing stains and disinfecting chopping boards, this chapter is chock-full of cleaning tips that are tough on dirt but kind to the environment.

This chapter explores ways to use your garden to lead a green lifestyle. Why not try growing some of your own food? Or setting up a compost heap? Composting diverts food waste from landfill and results in a fantastic soil improver. If you don't have space for a compost heap, you could try a wormery. There are lots of tips on fertilizing and getting rid of unwanted weeds and insects in an environmentally friendly way. Finally, if you are very keen, why not build a living roof and create a safe haven for plants and insects?

This chapter discusses why organic, Fairtrade, local and seasonal foods are environmentally friendly. It explores the issues around the rearing and treatment of animals in the production of meat and poultry. Including lots of tips for reducing, reusing and recycling food and food packaging; simple things such as writing a shopping list, making the most of leftovers and taking a lunch box to work instead of buying a cellophane-wrapped sandwich all make a difference.

Fashion & Beauty **154**

In this chapter, the issues surrounding the growth of textiles and the manufacturing of garments are explored. Again, the importance of reducing what you buy (by purchasing only what you need), reusing (by mending and tailoring), and recycling your clothes (by trading them with friends or donating them to a charity store) is discussed. Natural beauty products, including facemasks, shampoo and toothpaste, are offered as an alternative to the chemical-rich goods we most commonly use.

Celebrations **178**

Celebrate Christmas, birthdays, weddings and other occasions in an environmentally friendly way, from the gifts you give to the food you eat. Have you thought about buying an alternative gift, such as a goat for a farmer in a developing country? Try and ensure that the wrapping paper and greetings cards you use are reused and recycled. Alternatively, why not send an e-card? There are plenty of ways to enjoy yourself without placing an undue burden on the planet and its recourses.

Getting Around 194

Thinking about how we get around can have a great effect on our carbon footprint. Walking and cycling are free, increase fitness and do not produce any carbon emissions. Public transport and scooters only produce a small amount of carbon emissions. However, if you are wedded to the wheel, consider the type of car you drive; electric and hybrid cars are greener than large SUVs. The way you drive your car can also make a difference to the amount of fuel you use. Finally, give your vehicle a clean car wash.

Getting Away 214

Whilst long-haul travel is one of the most damaging activities for the environment, everyone needs a break. Have you considered a staycation, where you take a holiday in your own home?

There are alternatives to flying, such as taking the train, coach or ferry. Whilst it may take longer to get to your destination, the journey could be far more enjoyable. Alternatively, why not volunteer on vacation? You will experience a different way of life and contribute to the local community.

Work **230**

Don't leave your green principles behind every morning, try and save as much energy and water at work as you would in your own home. For example, switch off unused lights and don't leave your computer on standby. Including lots of ideas for saving resources such as paper and pens so you can start making your office a greener environment today.

Checklist **246**

Websites and Further Reading **252**

Index **254**

Foreword

Living a green life isn't just about being an ace recycler; it is a state of mind that can be liberating, empowering, cost-effective and a lot of fun.

We spend a lot of time procrastinating in an area of our lives that we know we need to change; we all know that once we have taken the first step, the sense of achievement makes the rest of the job seem a whole lot easier. I've seen thousands of people make the switch to living lives that are lighter on the planet and, without, exception everyone has commented on how easy it was to change, that none of it was rocket science and how they all wished they had done it years ago. Some were staggered by the amount of money they saved, and in these times of economic instability that is now a very big deal indeed.

This book is about the practical stuff, events and tasks and nice happenings that we encounter as part of our everyday lives. We all want to live greener, but with so much information out there it can be hard to decipher what really works. After all, time is our most precious resource, so we don't want to waste our efforts; this book is a great starting point, offering a little bit of clarity in a confusing world.

So many people ask me what the single most effective thing they could do to reduce their impact on the environment would be. When it comes down to it, the answer is very simple: just use less and share more. We always tell our kids to 'share nicely' and it really is time that we took that advice to heart. We are all aware that our natural resources are non-renewable, once they are gone, that's it – you can't get extra credit from the planet. As our global population continues to expand, we must accept that less means more for all in the long run.

Our grandparents lived in simpler times, when waste was considered bad taste and personal skills, such as sewing, growing and preserving food and many others, were a matter for pride. Such skills save a lot of money and make us more resilient; if you want to know how to live green, ask your gran!

Green is a wonderful colour, full of freshness and hope and life, but our lives are a rainbow of experience and every strand needs examining and refining to take our carbon footprint as low as we can. Fun, hope, love and laughter are all renewable sources of energy. Let's have a big green party, share the load and have a good time together!

Penney Poyzer
Green campaigner, broadcaster and author

Introduction

No-one can single-handedly save the world from global warming, pollution and diminishing resources. However, by actively choosing a greener lifestyle we can make a difference, and together we can achieve a great deal. By making green choices about how we live, we send clear messages to businesses and our elected political representatives that we want to preserve the health of our planet and everyone and everything that lives on it.

Defining Green Living

Do you have a 'bag for life'? Do you recycle? Do you eat organic food or drive a fuel-efficient car? All of these are green activities that make a difference to the health of our planet. In essence, going green means that we seriously consider our actions in order to minimize the negative impacts they have on our environment. We also make adjustments to our lifestyle and everyday habits to make positive impacts, even very small ones, so that the Earth will be able to support us, and future generations.

Benefits

Green living doesn't mean a drop in living standards. In fact, going green can mean an enhanced lifestyle; eliminating dangerous toxins from our homes, our foods and our environment can only be an improvement! Furthermore, if we don't take steps to green our lives, the effects of over-consumption, a throwaway culture and our quickly diminishing fossil fuel reserves *will* lead to serious falls in living standards!

Why Now?

Why go green now? Because there's no time like the present, and if we don't act now, there'll be no future.

Nothing New

Green thinking isn't new. Back in 1854, Henry David Thoreau published *Walden*, one of the earliest pieces of literature to address sustainable living. One hundred years later, Helen and Scott Nearing's book *Living the Good Life* (1954) kick-started the modern sustainable living movement, which gained momentum into the 1960s and 1970s. Although this was followed by a number of important works, including Donella Meadows' *The Limits to Growth* (1972) and E.F. Schumacher's *Small is Beautiful* (1973), many continued to ignore their messages.

Big Problems

In a rather perverse irony, it was the industrial age and modern technology itself that finally demonstrated to the world in no uncertain terms that we were facing a big problem; satellite technologies showed huge holes in the ozone layer and the devastation of oil slicks and water pollution. These were problems that weren't going to go away and that we could no longer afford to ignore. However, they were also problems that many realized could be solved at an individual level.

Sustainable and Renewable

At the heart of living green are the concepts of 'sustainability' and 'renewability'. Sustainability refers to using our resources in ways that satisfy our current needs without compromising the needs of future generations. It is often used in discussions about our current energy consumption because we are so highly dependent on the finite resources of oil and gas. These are not sustainable because we can't produce any more of them; when they're gone, they're gone for good. Renewable refers to a resource that can be produced again; examples include trees, which can be felled but replaced, and solar, wind and wave power, which will not run out.

Conscious Consumerism

In the past 20 years or so, we have finally begun to open our eyes to the devastation we are causing to our environment. We are realizing that if we don't change our ways, we are

pretty much doomed to existence on a dying planet. The initial problem was that while many wanted to help and make a difference, they didn't know how to live green lives. However, when consumers became aware that their pockets and purses had great power, the conscious consumer was born. Consumers can choose not to buy things that they do not need or that cause harm to the environment, as well as choosing to purchase products and services that are active in trying to make a difference.

Knowledge is Key

Knowledge is key to this process; consumers need to know where and how things are made or grown and where they end up, in order to make informed decisions and alter their consumption patterns.

What Next?

We live in a consumer society where our over-consumption is destroying the planet. If everyone in the world lived as we do, we'd need three planet Earths to sustain us. Despite the best efforts of space explorers, there aren't any other planets out there in our solar system that we can move to! The challenge today is for us to find practical ways to live and work at a sustainable level.

What More Can We Do?

Most people today probably recycle their newspapers or drinks cans with little inconvenience to their lives, while others have taken a more radical approach and have, for example, adopted a vegetarian or vegan diet. There are many, many ways in which we can all make our lives and our world a lot greener; some are simple, some take a little more effort, but they can all make a difference.

Save the World, and Some Money

If you're still not convinced that making a few changes to your lifestyle will save the world, then perhaps the fact that going green can save you money will be an encouragement.

Reducing consumption, reusing and recycling mean that you spend much less! It doesn't matter to greenies what your motivation is; as long as we all do something, we make a difference to the planet.

About This Book

This book is not the definitive textbook on green living. However, it is a good starting point for anyone who wants to make a difference. You don't have to quit the city and move to an eco-house in the country – unless you want to! Instead, try some of the small changes listed in this book; don't forget that small changes add up! You'll find that there are some things you already do, like recycling, but you will also find practical and straightforward ideas that you may not have thought of. Hopefully, these can help you become even greener, or enable you to become an even more informed and ethical consumer.

Start Greening Now

There's no better place to start going green than in the home. This book will show you how you can reduce the size of your carbon footprint and your domestic energy costs. There are sections on organic food and growing your own fruit and vegetables, on cleaning without poisoning yourself and the planet, and on green transport, where you can find out how to reduce your emissions and save fuel.

Everyone Can Live Green

Whether you are a family or a single person, a *gourmand* or a *fashionista*, stay-at-home parent or world traveller, you'll find useful, practical tips on how you can live a green lifestyle in this book. Best of all, you will make a vital contribution to saving our planet and improve your own wellbeing at the same time.

Waste & Unwanted Goods

Reduce

This is where it all starts: if we reduce the amount we buy, whether it's energy, food or consumer goods, we will reduce the amount we end up wasting and throwing away. In the United Kingdom alone, the average household spends over £400 a year on food that is thrown away uneaten because items are bought, not eaten and left to go off, or are cooked in too great a quantity for a meal and then thrown away. The USA and Japan both waste up to 50 per cent of all their food; Canadians throw out an estimated 30 million tonnes of food waste each year: that's enough food, according to Bob Lilienfeld, the co-author of *Use Less Stuff*, to feed the entire population of Canada! In Australia, 20 per cent of food purchased (worth a staggering AU$5.3 billion) is wasted each year: that's equivalent to buying five bags of groceries and throwing one bag away. We need to start rethinking our attitudes to buying and to wasting *all* our vital resources and to start considering where all this waste goes to!

The Bag for Life

Start reducing waste before you buy with a 'bag for life': many supermarkets and stores sell extra-strong, reusable shopping bags that they replace for free when they wear out. One simple, small investment will help to reduce the 10 billion plastic bags that are handed out at British supermarkets each year, the majority of which end up in landfill sites. Many towns and cities across the world such as San Francisco, USA, are now plastic-bag-free zones, and many more are set to follow San Francisco's lead.

Wrap Rage!

More than 18 per cent of all our household waste is made up of packaging from retail purchases. We can reduce this if we are prepared to make changes to our shopping habits, such as buying dry goods, produce and consumer durables loose rather than pre-packaged. More militant greens can also send a message to the supermarkets about unnecessary over-packaging: take your own containers with you and decant the produce into them after you've paid and leave the packaging behind. If there's a recycling facility on site, use it and save yourself an extra journey!

Think Once, Think Twice

Make this your mantra: it will help you make the distinction between a genuine *need* and a *want*. If you do *need* an item, consider whether it's the most energy-efficient, is rechargeable, is recyclable, or made of materials such as wood that have been guaranteed to come from a sustainable source. Don't be afraid to ask the retailer, and if they can't answer your questions, take your custom elsewhere. If you *want* an item, ask yourself why you want it and then if you really *need* it, and then ask yourself again!

Why Buy When You Can Rent?

You wouldn't buy the van to move your furniture to a new house, you'd rent it! Renting can be the ideal solution for items you will only use once or twice or for a short-term project. Instead of buying a chainsaw to cut down a dead tree in the garden, rent one instead. These days you can rent just about anything, from computers and carpet cleaners to cameras and even, designer handbags and jewellery, for a day, a week or longer. Check out the Internet for sites like www.erento.co.uk, www.zilok.com and www.azrental.co.uk, but check the details: some sites have an annual or monthly membership fee and commission fee on top of the hire fee.

Say No to Junk Mail

Fed up of junk mail, flyers and circulars? You can stop them from being delivered through your letterbox: put a sign on your door saying 'No Junk Mail'. It works pretty well, and any pizza menus that do make it through are generally from local establishments, so put them back through their letterbox as you pass! You can also sign up with various mailing preference services: this stops junk mail being delivered to your home via your postal service.

Measure Up

One of the easiest ways to reduce the amount we buy and waste is to make accurate measurements of the amounts we actually need. Measure once, measure twice, then write the numbers down clearly, specifying height, width and length where appropriate, so there are no errors and you won't buy more than you need. The same approach can be used for general shopping: 'Bogof' (buy one, get one free) offers, multi-packs and bulk-buying may save money, but can you carry it home and do you have the space to store it all? If you don't, go shopping with like-minded friends and split the costs on bulk-buy essentials!

Reuse

Investing in reusable, rechargeable or refillable products may involve an initial expense, but this is paid back over time. Even finding a secondary use for things is helpful: we've all reused screw-topped glass jars, so use your head and think inventively: the plastic-covered wire used for packaging the cords and leads on electrical appliances makes handy garden ties; old CDs and DVDs hung in vegetable patches keep the birds away; worn-out T-shirts cut into large squares make great dusters, and an odd sock can be slipped over the hand to make a useful polishing mitt!

What a Waste!

Wasted food is a waste of money and, when sent to landfill, is a major contributor to climate change because it breaks down to produce methane, which is a powerful greenhouse gas. Across the developed world, if we started reusing leftovers rather than throwing them away, it would have the same impact on carbon emissions as taking one in five cars off our roads!

Leftovers? What Leftovers?

According to environmental charity Waste Online, British households generate 3 million tonnes of food waste in the two-week period of Christmas alone. Each Christmas, Britons threw out £16 million worth of turkey, £40 million worth of cheese and £60 million worth of sausages: that's 1.2 million sausages for every day of the year! It's time to use the leftovers: for inspirational recipes, check out www.lovefoodhatewaste.com and start taking your lunch to work. There are some very easy ways to cut down on waste – all you have to do is shift your way of thinking.

Tips to Reduce Food Waste

Plan ahead: Start by thinking a little more long-term and plan out menus for a week. Make the shopping list you need to prepare the meals and stick to it when you go shopping.

Use leftovers: Think of leftovers not as waste but as another meal: today's chicken dinner is tomorrow's sandwich for lunch.

Try before you buy: If you fancy trying something new, try before you buy. This is a great way to introduce children to new flavours and textures. If you or they like it, then you know you can buy it and it won't be wasted.

Think portion control: The old saying 'our eyes are bigger than our stomachs' is true. Serve smaller portions and take a second helping if needed. Resist supersizing in restaurants, and if you can't eat it all, ask for a doggy bag to take it home!

Have set times for eating: This means you can ditch the between-meal snacks and be hungry for the main meal.

Beware of special offers on fresh and perishable foods: These are great if you are going to eat them straight away; if not, today's bargains can turn into tomorrow's waste.

Make Do and Mend

To make the most of reuse, we need to address our throwaway mentality. Before consigning anything to the bin, examine it carefully: most items (and this includes household items like computers, electrical equipment and furniture) can be repaired. Search for repair services in your local area online or in your phone book.

Have You Thought Of?
Using rechargeable batteries?

A Lick of Paint

You wouldn't move house because you're tired of the wallpaper, you'd redecorate instead. The same approach can be adopted to tired furniture: try sanding or stripping off the old paint or varnish (there are lots of products on the market that let you do this without

harming the environment or yourself, although you may have to use a little more elbow grease to get the results) then re-painting, varnishing or waxing. Upholstered furniture can be given a new lease of life with a good clean or some new covers. Some of the more simple makeovers, such as a removable, padded chair seat, you could do yourself with some attractive fabric. For large items you may need a professional's help: check in your local area for upholsterers and loose slip-cover makers.

Waste Not, Want Not

Reseal cans of paint by placing a stout piece of wood over the lid and hitting the wood with a hammer as you move it round the rim to ensure the lid is evenly secured. This helps to create an airtight seal, keeping the paint inside in pristine condition. For an even more airtight seal, smear a little petroleum jelly around the rim of the tin first. Store the paint tin upside down (mark the base of the tin with dab of colour to let you know what's inside) so that if a skin forms on the surface, when you turn the tin the right way up to remove the lid, the skin will be at the bottom. Alternatively, decant small quantities of leftover paint into screw-top glass jars: ideal for touching-up jobs. Label them with the colour name, maker and type of paint (water-based, solvent-based) and finish (matt, sheen or gloss) and store safely.

Like New

Just because the bristles have gone hard doesn't mean an old paintbrush can't be restored and reused. There are three valuable components in a paintbrush: the bristles (either natural or synthetic), the handle (wood or plastic) and the metal (holding the bristles to the handle) and, while all the components can be recycled, the costs of labour involved in disassembling them can be prohibitive, so they end up in landfills. Now, however, you can do your green bit: simmer the brush in vinegar until the bristles become soft; then scrape off any old paint with a nailbrush or wire brush. Wash the brush in warm soapy water, rinse and leave it to dry.

Recycle

It may not be the end of the consumer society but it's probably the end of the throwaway society, because we are running out of holes in the ground where we can hide our rubbish. Furthermore, the raw materials used to make things are valuable, some of the processes used in the manufacturing process are environmentally toxic, and non-renewable energy resources, such as coal, oil and gas, are in short supply. There are both environmental and economic imperatives for recycling still-serviceable items, or items which are stripped down to recover their component parts and materials.

One Can Make(s) A Big Difference

When a single aluminium soft-drink can is thrown away, it wastes the same amount of energy as if the can was half-filled with petrol (gasoline)! Recycling the can saves 96 per cent of the energy needed to make a new one, and it produces 95 per cent less air pollution and 97 per cent less water pollution. Put another way, recycling one soft drink can saves enough energy to run a light bulb continuously for a year!

Use the System

Most local governments and authorities operate household recycling schemes where the local council either provides centralized sites for disposal or collects recyclable household material. This valuable service means there is less fly-tipping and fewer items end up unnecessarily in landfill sites. If your local authority has this service, make sure you are using it – it'll save you the time and energy of having to take your waste to a certified disposal site.

What's Recycleable?

The answer to this is pretty much everything, but, for more specific answers, go to www.recyclenow.com. This will also tell you where your nearest recycling centres are. The recycling process consumes less energy – and therefore produces less carbon – than the extraction and processing of new raw materials.

Recycling Reminders

 Visual reminders: Make a note on your calendar or fridge door as a visual reminder of the days/dates that your recycling is collected.

 Whole house recycling: We're getting used to recycling in the kitchen, but don't overlook the other rooms in your house. If you can recycle plastic bottles, then make sure they all go in the recycling bin, including shampoo, shower gel and household cleaning bottles.

 Keep it simple: Put your recycling bin next to your main bin: that way you'll only need to make one trip to empty the trash. If you don't have a recycling bin and a doorstep collection is available in your area, contact your local council for one.

 Follow the guidelines: Each region collects recycling material in different ways. Some want newspaper and paper waste separate from cans and glass; some don't take cardboard cartons or plastic drinks bottles. Find out how your local system operates and follow the rules so all your recycling waste is taken away and reused.

Charity Begins at Home

Charity stores play a vital role in recycling, and your donations support their work at home and abroad. You can also shop around and select your favourite charity to support, be it animal welfare, education, community support, mental health or research into medicine. Clothes are the number one donation (and purchase) and those that aren't sold in stores can be sent abroad, or sold to textile agents for large-scale recycling into stuffing for new sofas.

Bric-a-Brac and Furniture

Household items are expensive to purchase new and there are many families and individuals who rely on second-hand or free items to help furnish their homes. Freecycle (see later in the chapter) is a great way to recycle unwanted goods and pass on useful items to new owners. Check online and in your phone book, too, for local charity or community groups like the Furniture Recycling Network who will collect furniture for redistribution (but note that while they will take bed frames, they will not take used mattresses; these will have to be disposed of through your local council).

Well-read

Recent copies of magazines and comic books are always welcome in doctors', dentists' and vets' waiting rooms, so pass them on.

Collective Action

Get active in your local community! Your local newspaper will probably have listings of groups like swap shops, which are great for children and teenagers who want to meet and swap books, comics, video and computer games. If you have a close-knit community of neighbours then why not get together and pool resources: trade and borrow items among your community, hire a skip together in spring for a bulk clear-out or make a community notice board to advertise items for sale or exchange.

The Eyes Have It!

Fashion and design companies have made a mint out of licensing their names to be placed on products such as spectacles. Because these are now marketed as fashion items, spectacles go out of fashion, so there's probably a pair (or two) that just won't be worn again. If you've got any old spectacles that you don't use tucked away in a drawer, then you have the gift of sight in your hands. For some people in the world's poorest countries, being able to see to read or sew means being able to continue working to support themselves and their families. Charities such as VisionAid and Sightsavers International have teamed up with high-street chains of opticians (in the UK, Specsavers is part of the scheme) to accept old spectacles for use in developing countries.

Mobile Phones

The trend to upgrade mobile phones means that thousands, if not millions, of perfectly serviceable mobile phones are tucked away into drawers. These can be passed on, and many retailers operate schemes where, if you hand in your old handset for recycling, you get some cash back. But you can do better: charity organizations are delighted to accept old handsets for recycling, meaning you are effectively donating your cash back to a good cause. Other aid organizations specialize in sending mobile phones to developing countries to be distributed to community health workers, farming and trading co-operatives. Many of the big retailers have freepost envelopes at the checkouts that enable you to send your phone off to a reuse scheme.

This Does Not Compute!

No-one wants an old computer, do they? Oh yes they do! If you've upgraded your PC or laptop or bought a new flat-screen monitor or keyboard and mouse, then there are number of organizations, such as www.computeraid.org, who will relieve you of your old equipment and make it serviceable (they'll remove any and all of your data and software) before passing it on to charities at home or abroad. This makes more sense than sending it to a landfill site.

Printer Cartridges

In Britain alone, an estimated 350 million ink cartridges are sent to landfill sites every year. To cut down on the volume of waste:

 Only print when necessary: If you must print, use both sides of the paper.
 Buy only refillable cartridges.
 Recycle old cartridges.

E-cycling Schemes

Many of the big IT retailers have charity envelopes so you can send cartridges by freepost or, find details of recycling schemes for IT equipment online. Schemes run by organizations such as Reclaim IT in the UK will recycle printer cartridges on behalf of Oxfam. Reclaim IT will also provide a box for your workplace or office for old mobiles, laser printer cartridges and inkjet cartridges. Wherever you live, get online and search out reuse and recycling schemes in your area. E-cycling schemes, which recycle electronic equipment such as computers, scanners and printers, either for their component parts and metals (for reuse) or for use in developing countries, are a great way to dispose of items following a home or office upgrade.

Garage and Table-Top Sales

Here's a way to find new homes for unwanted items and make a bit of spare cash as well: organize a garage or a table-top sale at your home. Go though your home, including the attic, cellar, shed and garage, and have a good clear-out. Decide on a reasonable price and label everything you want to sell, but be prepared to drop prices for hagglers!

Car Boot Sales

Car boot sales have grown in popularity over the past decade; they even spawned a number of television programmes about boot-fair treasure hunters. Vendors usually pay a fee, which can vary depending on site location, popularity and whether your boot is a car or a van. But remember, like a table-top or garage sale, what remains unsold at the end of the day is *your* responsibility: you have to take it home with you again!

Good To Go

Whether you use a table-top, garage or car boot sale, eBay, Freecycle, a charity store or any other recycling scheme, make sure that everyone in your household has agreed that it's alright for it to go – don't assume that because Auntie Ethel never uses an item, she doesn't want it. And don't recycle your flatmate's stuff just because it's getting on your nerves; it may have significance or value for them!

On the Internet

The Internet presents loads of opportunities for recycling unwanted goods, and sometimes making a bit of money too!

eBay

Most people have heard of eBay, but many don't realize that individuals can both buy and sell items on it. eBay is a great way to recycle unwanted or excess goods – and get paid, too!

Amazon Marketplace

When you buy a book on Amazon, you are offered the choice of buying it new or used at considerably reduced prices. On Amazon, you can list your own book that you want to sell: you just set your price (it's not an auction like eBay) and there's no need for a photo. Second-hand books will be listed for around 80 days but you can re-register them at the click of a button. Do be aware that Amazon adds a set amount for postage, so you may need to add something to the price to cover this. Check the selling price of other books already listed to see if your copy is worth listing.

Freecycle

The Freecycle Network began in 2003 in Tucson, Arizona. Today, Freecycle is made up of over 4,500 groups with more than 6 million members worldwide. It's a grassroots and entirely non-profit-making movement of people who are giving (and getting) stuff for free in their local areas, with each group moderated by a local volunteer. Freecycle is all about reusing and recycling and keeping waste (about 500 tonnes a day) out of landfill sites.

Another Man's Treasure

Freecycle is easy to use: you can post messages about the things you don't want, someone local contacts you to say they want it, and they come and collect it! That's it! Simple, yet very effective and worthwhile.

In a Jiffy

Jiffy bags are the padded envelopes stuffed with shredded cardboard rather than plastic bubble wrap, but you can easily recycle *all* types of padded envelopes: first, you could keep them for yourself and reuse them, or you can advertise them on Freecycle. You'll find someone who'll be very grateful for them.

The Green Consumer

Going green does not mean that we leave the modern world behind; we still have to buy things, but we can now make decisions about the type of products we buy, based on factors such as energy efficiency, use of sustainable or recycled materials and ethical production and trade. Increasingly, manufacturers have responded to growing consumer awareness of environmental issues and ethical concerns and realized this is not just a trend but absolutely vital if they want their companies to survive in the future. From new-build houses and big-ticket items, like cars and electrical appliances, to bars of chocolate, a growing range of products is available to the concerned consumer.

Fairtrade

One of the best known ethical schemes is Fairtrade. Fairtrade is all about better prices, decent working conditions, local sustainability and fair terms of trade for farmers and workers in the developing world. Because it requires companies to pay sustainable prices (which must never fall lower than the market price), the scheme is able to address some of the injustices of conventional trade, which traditionally discriminates against the poorest, weakest producers. Fairtrade enables them to improve their position and have more control over their lives. The range of Fairtrade products includes over 3,000 products, such as coffee, tea, cocoa and chocolate, as well as fruit, cotton, cut flowers, herbs and spices, nuts and oils.

How Green is Your Money?

When you put your money in the bank, it gets invested in order to make interest and a profit: but you may be alarmed at where your current bank is investing your money! It may be being used to fund loans to companies that do animal testing, don't pay fair wages to their employees internationally, violate human rights, are polluters or even support repressive political regimes. You may only have a small amount of money in the bank, but if you add up all the pennies, they soon turn into millions of pounds, dollars, and euros! Some banks do, however, operate according to an environmental and/or ethical policy: in the UK, the Cooperative Bank and its online 'sister' Smile consider the wider implications of their investments. Triodos Bank only invests in ethical projects and also works with a number of charities, as does Citizens Bank in Canada.

Investing in Green Growth

There are a number of ethical investment funds available that operate on the principle of not investing any money in any enterprise that would harm the environment, people around the world or flora and fauna. The money you invest is in turn only invested in green companies that can prove their credentials. These investments are called SRIs (Socially Responsible Investments) or Ethical Investments, and your money is pooled with that of other investors to buy shares in green companies. As with non-green unit trusts, you make money as the value of the shares grows, but you can also lose money if the value of the shares goes down. There are two different shades of green: light green and dark green. The darker green the fund, the stricter the rules that govern what the fund can be invested in. The Ethical Investment Research Service (EIRIS) is a charity that provides independent research into the behaviour of thousands of companies. The EIRIS website at www.eiris.org not only has a list of ethical investment advisors and FAQs, but you can also check to see just how light or dark green a company is before you decide whether you want your money invested there.

Money Talks

If you decide to switch to an ethical bank, tell your current bank why you are switching. Your actions may tip the balance in favour of them rethinking some of their policies. Do note, though, that ethical banks generally work with smaller profit margins than the big-name banks, so they may have fewer offices and operate largely by phone, post and the Internet.

Checklist

- **Think of the 'Three Rs'**: Reduce, Reuse and Recycle and make them part of you and your family's everyday routine.

- **Get a 'bag for life'**: Reduce the number of shopping bags you use.

- **Make the most of leftovers**: Reuse food for lunches or another meal.

- **Does your local area have a recycling service?**: If so, find out what they collect and make the most of it.

- **Find new homes for your unwanted belongings**: At garage sales, car boot sales or over the Internet.

- **Think about the source of items you buy**: Make a point of buying ethically and sustainably produced, recycled and recyclable goods wherever possible.

- **Investigate green bank accounts and investments**: Put your money where your mouth and your beliefs are.

Energy & Water

First Steps: Calculate Your Carbon Footprint

A carbon footprint is the total amount of CO_2 (carbon dioxide) and other greenhouse gas emissions caused directly or indirectly by each individual, organization, event or product. A carbon footprint is usually expressed as a CO_2 equivalent, such as the CO_2 emissions for cars of different engine sizes. There are a number of ways in which carbon footprints are measured, but it is possible to get a good idea of your household's footprint size by calculating the amount of energy used in the home, on travel and other activities: www.carbonfootprint.com has an online calculator and will give you an idea of where, and how, you can make changes to your lifestyle to reduce emissions.

Offsetting

Over 40 per cent of the current carbon dioxide emissions come from the things that we do every day. Leaving the lights on, leaving electrical equipment on standby or over-filling the kettle not only waste energy (and money) but also result in needless CO_2 emissions. Offsetting (one of the new century's buzzwords) is a way in which individuals and businesses can compensate for carbon emissions by investing in offset companies, which in turn invest in projects that will reduce carbon emissions by an equal amount to what has been emitted.

Offsetting Projects

The most common types of carbon reduction projects include renewable energies such as wind farms, biomass energy and hydroelectric schemes, as well as reforestation projects. Carbon offsetting, as part of a carbon-neutral lifestyle, has gained momentum among consumers as awareness and concern grows regarding the potentially negative environmental effects of our energy-intensive lifestyles and economies. The Kyoto Protocol sanctioned carbon offsetting as a way in which governments, business and individuals could earn carbon credits that can be traded on a marketplace, such as the Chicago Climate Exchange. This led to the Clean Development Mechanism (CDM), which validates and measures projects to ensure they produce actual benefits and are genuine. The CDM Gold Standard identifies offset projects that:

 Meet sustainable standards.
 Deliver benefits to local communities.
 Are based on energy efficiency or renewable energy.

Save Energy

Energy offsetting *doesn't* mean you never have to worry about saving energy: you do! The most effective way to help fight climate change is to *cut* the amount of energy used and *reduce* our personal carbon footprint.

Read the Carbon Label

Carbon labelling was introduced in 2007 in the UK by The Carbon Trust. Having started life as an experiment, carbon labelling is now being rolled out across the world with schemes launched in the United States and Canada, Europe and Asia. A carbon label shows the total amount of CO_2 emitted during every stage of an item's production and distribution (its carbon footprint). At the moment, different countries calculate product carbon footprints (or PFCs) in slightly different ways, creating potential confusion for the consumer.

The Green Index

Many businesses are now calling for an international standard for carbon labelling, such as the Green Index rating system pioneered by the footwear company Timberland in conjunction with The Carbon Trust. The Green Index product label ranks selected Timberland products according to the emissions created during production, the presence of hazardous substances and the percentage or organic and renewable materials. Unfortunately, as more individual carbon label standards are developed, a single, universal standard is still some way off but, in the meantime, as more manufacturers sign up for the various schemes, consumers will at least be able to make more informed decisions about their purchases and feel that it's not just them doing all the work to help improve the environment.

Energy-efficient Homes

The best place to start reducing your carbon footprint is in the home. A few simple but cost-effective changes can radically lower the amount of energy used in heating your home and water, meaning less wasted energy and more money in your wallet. Some measures, such as fitting low-energy bulbs, take just a few minutes; others are easy DIY projects like draught-proofing and insulating; and a few may need some additional support from a skilled professional, but all will make a difference. Making your home energy-efficient can save you up to £300 ($500 US) a year.

What's the Difference?

A great deal! The average household could save around 1.5 tonnes of CO_2 just by making their home more energy-efficient. If every household in the UK installed just *one* energy-efficient

light bulb, the amount of CO_2 emissions saved would be enough to fill the Royal Albert Hall in London over 2,000 times! If every American home replaced just one ordinary light bulb with an energy-efficient one, the US would save enough energy to light more than three million homes for a year and prevent greenhouse gas emissions equivalent to 800,000 cars.

Energy-efficient Light Bulbs

Switching to energy-efficient light bulbs means:

- **Lower energy bills**: Low-energy bulbs use up to 75 per cent less energy than conventional incandescent ones.
- **Fewer purchases**: Low-energy bulbs last up to ten times longer than conventional ones.
- **They are safer**: Low-energy bulbs produce 75 per cent less heat than ordinary ones so they are safer to operate; they can also cut energy costs in summer when cooling systems are needed.
- **Range of sizes and shapes**: Low-energy bulbs are available in a range of sizes and shapes to fit almost any fixture for indoor and outdoor use.

Turn It Off

The cheapest and easiest way to reduce both your energy bills and your carbon footprint is to turn off all appliances when they are not in use. Leaving appliances plugged in and switched on at the socket means they're still using energy, so turn off mobile phone and laptop chargers, TVs and games consoles when they're not being used.

Insulation

Home-energy use is responsible for over a quarter of all CO_2 emissions. Cutting down on energy used and reducing the amount of wasted energy will not only help tackle climate change but save you money as well, so it's a win-win situation. The the majority of buildings don't have the recommended amount of insulation which means that heat escaping from our homes is costing us money!

Wrap Up

A surprising number of homes have hot water tanks without insulating jackets, perhaps because the tank is 'out of sight, out of mind' in the attic or loft. Get up there and put a jacket on the tank: they cost very little and, with the heat it traps, it will pay for itself in under six months. You need to fit one that's at least 75 mm (3 in) thick.

Loft Insulation

Around half of all the heat in our homes is lost through the roof and walls. Insulating your loft is easy to do, relatively cheap and you can do it yourself. Even if you already have some insulation, it's worth checking it: in the UK it needs to be the recommended 270 mm (just over 10½ in) thickness. If your loft insulation isn't this thick, add another layer! In the United States, homeowners can check out the US Department of Energy's website as each state (and indeed local codes) specifies minimum insulation requirements depending on climatic conditions in each area.

Insulation Materials

While installing insulation makes a difference to the amount of energy wasted, the most widely used loft insulation materials are not especially green. The two main types of insulation are mineral fibre or glass-fibre matting (which comes on rolls about 400 mm (16 in) wide), and loose-fill pellets made of mineral fibre, vermiculite and cellulose. While easy for DIYers to install, both can irritate the skin and throat and need to be handled with care. You even have to wash any clothes worn after installation to remove stray fibres.

Green Insulation

There are natural and recycled alternatives which are non-toxic and non-irritant: Warmcel 100 is made from recycled paper; Isonat from hemp and recycled cotton; and Thermafleece and Black Mountain are both made from sheep's wool. While the initial cost of these green alternatives may be higher, they do have significant advantages over mineral fibre insulation:

 More thermally efficient.

 Use less energy and emit less CO_2 in their manufacture.

 Safer to handle.

 Able to absorb and release moisture: Without losing efficiency.

 Can store CO_2 during growth: In the case of hemp.

 Can be composted or incinerated: At the end of its (long) life.

Within These Walls

Around a third of heat lost in a house without insulation will have escaped through the walls. If your home was built after 1920, then the chances are it has cavity walls: external walls made up of two layers with a small gap (cavity) between them. Insulating the cavity by filling the gap saves energy, keeps the heat in, reduces CO_2 emissions and, in some instances, helps reduce condensation inside the house. The major utility suppliers can provide subsidised installation under the Carbon Emissions Reduction Target (CERT) and there are also grants available for households with particular needs or on low incomes.

Up Against a Wall

Houses built before 1920 are generally of a solid wall construction. While older houses may look good, their construction often means that their walls leech even more heat than unfilled cavity walls. The only way to reduce the heat loss is to insulate the walls, either on the outside (which may dramatically alter the house's appearance and be prohibited if it's listed, of historic interest or in a conservation area) or on the inside. Interior-wall insulation is available in ready-made form and usually consists of plasterboard laminates or wooden battens in-filled with insulation. They are generally about 90 mm (3½ in) thick. So while you save heat and cut costs (a three-bedroom, semi-detached house with internal wall insulation saves around 2.4 tonnes of CO_2 a year), you do lose some room space.

Get a Grant

Some households are eligible for grants towards the cost of bringing their insulation up to scratch. Depending on your household circumstances, you may not even have to pay anything: utility providers and local governments both bear the responsibility and the costs. Check the offers from each and remember you don't have to be a customer of a particular gas or electricity provider for them to arrange the installation of insulation as it is a government requirement that they do so. At the moment, non-green insulation materials are the only types offered under the various different government grant and discount schemes.

Dodge the Draught

Cold air entering through gaps around doors and windows means warm air is also escaping. Cheap, self-adhesive, draught-excluding strips, PVC or brush door-seals are easy to fix. Keyholes also allow cold air to race in; fit escutcheons or covers where possible, and if you can't, just make a 'bung' by tying a piece of rope into a knot so it fits in the hole! Tie it in a longish piece of rope and fasten it to the handle – that way it won't get mislaid.

Snakes and Sausages

You can call them what you like, but fabric or knitted tubes stuffed with wadding make for terrific draught excluders and tackle the bases or doors. They're simple and cheap to assemble, and make a real difference. And don't forget the letterbox: the single exterior flap is not enough to keep out draughts, so fit an interior flap and make a sausage to fit in the void.

Curtains Up

One of the simplest ways to keep heat indoors is to close the curtains before dusk. The heavier the curtain fabric, the more insulation you have and the cosier you'll be. Door curtains are also beneficial, whether the door is solid wood or part or fully glazed. You can buy what are known in the trade as drapery arms for door curtains: these are curtain poles that are hinged at one end so the whole curtain swings back when you open the door.

Double Vision

Double glazing is a major investment, especially as most companies will encourage you to replace every door and window in your home. While installing full double glazing will save the average three-bedroom home from emitting about 700 kg (around 1,500 lbs) of CO_2 a year (as double glazing cuts heat loss through windows by about half), the costs can be prohibitive, especially if you have non-standard sized windows, or prefer wooden frames to uPVC ONES. An alternative is to look at the rooms that cost the most to heat and replace the windows in these.

Secondary Glazing

If your home is listed, of historic interest or in a conservation area, changing the windows may not be appropriate. An option is to install secondary glazing: these are usually a series of horizontal sliding sashes installed inside the existing windows to block out draughts coming through gaps around sashes and between the walls and window frame.

DIY Glazing

A cheaper, but more temporary, alternative to double or secondary glazing is to buy a DIY film-glazing kit. They are simple to install: double-sided tape is stuck around the window frame and the film stuck to the tape. The film is shrunk to fit tightly across the frame using the heat from a hair dryer. While you can't open the window without removing the film, this solution can be ideal for the winter months (or if you are in rented accommodation) and works better than cling film.

Extractor Fans

Many apartment conversions have bathrooms squeezed in between rooms and that means they often don't have a window for light or ventilation. Instead, when the bathroom light is switched on, an extractor fan generally powers up. While they are a legal requirement under building regulations, extractor fans are noisy and if you leave it switched on in the bathroom with the door open for one hour, it will suck all the heated air out of an average one-bedroom flat. Instead of wasting energy (you don't need the extractor fan to brush your teeth), fit a battery-operated light (with a rechargeable battery, of course) and use the extractor only when you have a bath or shower to remove the steam.

Heating the Home

Saving energy while we heat our homes is a priority: it not only saves the planet but it also saves money. You can only be in one room at a time, so take control of your heating! Do you really need to be heating the hallway, bathroom or even the bedrooms when you are not in them? When everyone is out of the house, switch off your heating to avoid warming an empty house.

Boiler Emissions

Gas central heating boilers account for around 60 per cent of the CO_2 emissions in a gas-heated home. High-efficiency condensing boilers, along with improved heating controls, will significantly cut the amount of CO_2 emissions and save money, as they are more efficient. The lifespan of a boiler is around 15 years, so if you are planning to replace or upgrade your central heating system, choosing a high-efficiency condensing boiler with the correct heating controls can make a enormous difference to your heating bills over time. There may be grants and offers available to help you install an energy-efficient heating system; ask your local authority or utility supplier for details of grants and energy efficiency schemes.

Energy-efficient Boilers

In the UK, boilers have a rating displayed as the SEDBUK label. This stands for the Seasonal Efficiency of Domestic Boilers in the UK, and provides a basis for fair comparison of different boiler models by arranging boilers into bands according to their efficiency. SEDBUK rates boilers on a scale of A to G: band A is the most efficient and band G the least efficient, so look on the labels.

Condensing Boilers

A high-efficiency condensing boiler works on the principle of recovering as much as possible of the waste heat that is normally wasted from the flue of a conventional (non-condensing) boiler. The best high-efficiency condensing boilers convert more than 90 per cent of their fuel into heat, compared to 78 per cent for conventional types.

Take Control of Your Heating

Heating controls will keep your home at a comfortable temperature, making it warm when you want it but switching the heating off when you don't. They include: a programmer, a room thermostat, a combined programmable room thermostat, a cylinder thermostat and thermostatic radiator valves (TRVs).

On and Off

Heating controls allow you to choose when the heating is on, how warm it is, and where you want the warmth. They will also make sure that the boiler is only turned on when it needs to be. A well-controlled heating system should have:

 A timer/programmer.
 A room thermostat.

(Combined programmable room thermostats, instead of separate programmer and room thermostat are also available.)

 A cylinder thermostat: If your home has a regular condensing boiler with a hot-water cylinder.
 Thermostatic radiator valves (TRVs).

Set the Timer

Timers or programmers allow you to set when the heating and/or hot water come on and go off. This way, you heat your home and hot water only as and when you need to, saving both energy and money.

Room Thermostat

A room thermostat constantly measures the air temperature of a room and can be set to whatever temperature suits you best: ideally between 18 and 21° C (64–69° F). The best position to locate one is in the room that is occupied the most often. When the temperature falls below the setting, the thermostat switches on the central heating; and once the room reaches the set temperature, the thermostat switches the heating off.

Hot-Water Cylinder Thermostat

If you don't have a combi boiler (a tankless system), a cylinder thermostat keeps a constant check on the temperature of the water in a hot-water cylinder. The cylinder thermostat switches the heat supply from the boiler on and off as required to keep the water at a set temperature. Installing a cylinder thermostat can reduce CO_2 emission from the home by110 kg (242 lbs) a year.

Too Hot to Handle

Water doesn't have to be boiling hot; you'd have to use more cold water to cool it down. Set your hot-water cylinder thermostat at 60° C (140° F) – any higher is a waste of energy (and water) and can lead to scalding; any lower and there may be risks of legionella.

Thermostatic Radiator Valves (TRVs)

TRVs can help you save money and energy, and around 45 kg (100 lbs) of CO_2 a year, as they allow different temperatures in different rooms, and they let you turn the heating off completely in rooms that aren't used. TRVs work by sensing the air temperature around them and regulating the flow of hot water entering the radiators to keep a set temperature in a room. Radiators in the space containing the room thermostat should not normally have a TRV, but if they do, keep the TRV on its highest setting, and set the room thermostat to the required temperature instead.

Have You Thought Of?

If you are out of the house all day then your heating shouldn't need to be switched on. Set the timer/programmer so the heating comes on a little time before you return home; it will be nice and warm for your arrival.

Hot Tips for Heating

☑ **Make sure thermostats are not covered**: Programmable thermostats, room thermostats and TRVs all need a free flow of air to sense the temperature. Make sure they are not covered by curtains or blocked by furniture and note that nearby sources of heat (such as lamps) can also stop them from sensing the room temperature correctly.

☑ **Your home will take a while to cool down**: If you are out of the house during the day, set your heating (and hot water) to switch off before you leave in the morning. In the evening, set your heating to switch off before you go to bed: this means you're not heating the house while you're asleep.

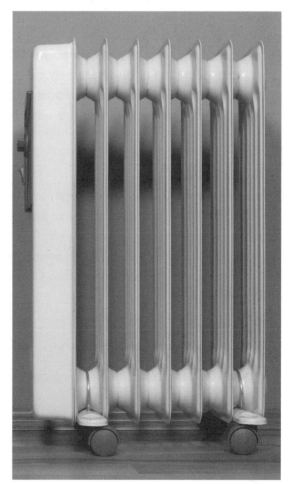

☑ **Bleed your radiators**: Bleeding your radiators removes unwanted air from the heating system. This will keep your radiators working at their maximum output. (Switch off the heating system when you do this so that more air isn't drawn into the system.)

☑ **Insulate your central heating and hot water pipes**: Especially those between your boiler and hot-water cylinder.

Appliances, Gadgets and Gizmos

Home is where the heart is and where a great deal of energy is used and, unfortunately, wasted. Simple measures like switching lights off in rooms that aren't being used, turning electrical appliances off completely (and not leaving them on standby) and switching to low-energy light bulbs and energy-efficient appliances are easy to do and save money.

Smart Meter

A good way to assess your existing electrical energy use is to buy a smart meter. They're simple to use and operate by battery: you put a magnet on your live feed at the electricity meter and use a wireless monitor to read your usage in any room in the house. The smart meter will tell you your electricity usage (in power units or in the financial cost) and updates the information every five seconds. Switch on a light or the kettle and watch the meter empty your wallet!

Let There Be Light

If you haven't made the switch to low-energy bulbs, then now is the time: they are now significantly cheaper than when they were first introduced and some utilities companies even have free ones to give away, so contact them. Turn room lights out when not in use and ask yourself if you need a light in a cupboard! Mean greens may even remove the light bulb from the fridge or freezer to save energy!

Kitchen Appliances

The modern kitchen has numerous hi-tech appliances; these mean many ways of wasting, or saving energy.

Fridges and Freezers

Together these are two of the biggest energy consumers in our homes, on the go 24 hours a day, seven days a week, so you need to make sure that they are running at their most efficient. The first check is to make sure the doors close tightly: if the seals are worn or damaged, then cold air is escaping and warm air is getting in, making the appliance work harder (and consuming more energy) to keep the contents chilled or frozen. Put a piece of paper in the door and close it: any slippage of the paper means the seals aren't tight enough.

A+ For Energy Efficiency

When you buy a new fridge or freezer (or a combination), look for the energy rating label: those marked A+ are more energy-efficient than A-rated products. For refrigeration, European Union energy labels go up to A++. In other parts of the world, equivalent energy-efficiency and star-rating systems are also in use: in Australia, washing machines and dryers, dishwashers, fridges, freezers and air-conditioners carry energy labels, while other products such as hot-water heaters carry minimum energy performance (MEP) labels. In the USA, the Environmental Protection Agency (EPA) and Department of Energy run the programme called Energy Star, which labels consumer goods (and new homes) according to their energy efficiency.

Space Means Waste

Keep your fridge and freezer well-stocked: spaces mean that the appliance has to work to circulate the cold air over a larger area. If there are spaces in your fridge, put some containers of water in it; in the freezer, fill the gaps with scrunched-up plastic bags.

Defrost

If you've got a polar ice cap in your freezer or freezer compartment, it needs defrosting. Check that the temperature control is not set too high, and defrost on a regular basis.

Kettles

Kettles are one of the most frequently used domestic appliances. Kettles that are labelled 'Energy Saving Recommended' (in the UK) have to meet strict testing criteria to demonstrate that they use 20 per cent less energy than an ordinary kettle. If everyone switched to an energy-efficient kettle, we would save enough energy to power over 300,000 homes for an entire year. And if everyone only boiled up enough water for one or two cups of tea or coffee rather than filling the kettle to the top, the reduction in energy used over one year would equal the output that a typical power station produces over four months.

Have You Thought Of?

Descaling the kettle? It will work better, faster and more efficiently and last longer.

Washing Machines

The most energy-efficient washing machines are rated AAA: A for energy efficiency, A for wash quality and A for spin, and use a third less energy than older washing machines. Wash full loads rather than half loads: that way you'll use less energy and less water. You can also drastically reduce the number of times you use the washing machine by opting to hand-wash small items instead.

Tumble Dryers

Tumble dryers guzzle energy, contributing a staggering 0.15 tonnes of CO_2 emissions per year. If it is practical and permitted, then why not peg your washing out on the line? Your clothes will smell gorgeous, and wind and sunshine are free! You could also consider investing in a pulley-operated clothes airer. Made from wood and cast iron, it is usually attached to the ceiling and is capable of holding up to 30 kg (66 lbs) of laundry. Perfect for rainy days and for those with no outside space, it may make your tumble dryer redundant.

Dishwashers

Like washing machines, dishwashers should only be run with a full load, so you can either live with a kitchen full of dirty dishes for a an extra day or two, or perhaps think about sensible washing-up by hand!

Microwaves

Some people love them, some hate them, but microwave ovens are more energy-efficient than conventional electric or gas ovens and are therefore cheaper to use and more environmentally friendly. Note that a digital timer is more accurate (and consequently safer) for cooking than an analogue dial timer.

Kitchen Energy Tips

- **Shut that door**: Every time you open the oven door, you lower the temperature inside by 25 per cent. When you close the door, the oven has to use more energy to bring the temperature back up to the desired heat level. The same is true for fridges and freezers, but in reverse. Electric ovens can have the heat turned off ten minutes before the end of cooking; if you keep the door closed, there will be enough heat to finish the cooking process.

- **Use the right-sized ring for the pan**: The hottest part of a flame is the tip, so the flames should not be shooting up the sides of pans! Use the smallest ring if you are simmering or slow-cooking.

- **Put a lid on it**: Cooking in pans with lids reduces energy use: the heat stays in the pan! If you need to let off steam and there's no escape hole in the lid, then pop a (used) matchstick or cocktail stick beneath the lid to raise it a little.

- **Wash clothes on the lowest temperature setting you can**: And make sure you have a full load.

- **Choose a fridge with a freezer on top**: This is more energy-efficient than two separate appliances.

- **Look at the Energy Efficiency Label**: Introduced in 1995, by law (UK), all refrigeration appliances, washing machines and tumble dryers, dishwashers, electric ovens, lamps and light bulb packaging must display this information.

That's Entertainment!

As broadcasters switch over to digital broadcasting, most people will use the opportunity to upgrade their old TV set. Be warned though – while they look good, plasma screen TVs use up to five times more energy than the old box. Leaving the TV, DVD, music centre, games console or portable radio on 'standby' means it's still using power: that little green or red light is wasting energy! The latest IDTVs (Integrated Digital TVs) can be switched off completely without losing any of their settings, so there's no need for standby mode.

DAB Radios

While DAB (Digital Audio Broadcasting) radio manufacturers are keen to tell us about their crystal-clear sound, what's not so well known is the fact that DAB radios consume more energy. Even on standby they use about 5 W of energy, which is about five times higher than analogue radios.

Computers and Screens

It's the screen/monitor that consumes the most power in a computer; look to your screen settings and set it to sleep mode if you don't use the computer for more than two minutes. During longer breaks and at the end of the day, switch the monitor off completely. Power off computers when not in use, and when they are, why not use a USB charger? Two AA rechargeable batteries can be recharged from your computer while you work, surf the net or play games. If you use a laptop or notebook, the mains supply should be switched off when the battery is full: once charged, a battery can't accept any more power, but the power is still being fed through and wasted. Looking after the battery will extend its life, and so will checking your power-save options for it: you can usually choose and switch between better battery life or better performance. If you are just running one programme, such as word processing a document, then opt for better battery life.

Power to the People

Most of our energy comes from burning fossil fuels (coal and gas) and, because neither are renewable sources, they will eventually run out. Burning fossil fuels is also a major contributor to climate change. Carbon-free sources of energy include nuclear power and renewable or green energy (hydro, wind, solar and biomass power). You can find out just how green your electricity supply is by going online and using the energy comparison websites. If you live in the USA, you can use the EPA's 'Power Profiler': enter your zip code and electricity supplier and you'll see which sources are used.

Green Energy

Most of the energy suppliers offer green electricity, which seeks to support the use of renewable sources, but they may all do it in different ways. The two main types are green supply tariffs and green funds.

Green Supply Tariffs

This means that some or all of the electricity you buy is matched by purchases of renewable energy that the supplier makes on your behalf. The energy may come from a range of energy sources such as a hydroelectricity plant or a wind farm. When you opt for a green supply tariff, your energy supplier should inform you about what sources are included in the mix and what proportion is renewable.

Green Energy Funds

A green fund normally involves the consumer paying a premium to contribute to a fund that will be used to support new renewable energy projects and developments, but the energy supplied to you will be continued on your existing tariff. Although the cost of producing energy from renewables is slightly higher than non-renewable sources, your contributions now will help to swing the balance in favour of renewable energy sources in the future.

Turning the Switch to Green

Because there are a number of green energy offerings available in the market and each supports the use of renewable power in different ways, before you decide to switch to green energy, you may want to consider the following:

 Cost: Will it cost more than my current tariff?

Type: Is it a green tariff, a green fund or a different sort of offering?

 Proportion: What proportion of your green supply tariff will come from renewable sources?

 Independently verified: Is there an independent body that verifies the supplier's green offerings and claims?

Green Fuels

Unlike fossil fuels, renewable fuels are what they say they are: renewable. They won't run out, and they will reduce CO_2 emission and meet our energy requirements. Biomass (sometimes known as biofuels or bioenergy) is produced from living or recently dead organic material, either directly from plants (such as ethanol derived from sugar cane) or indirectly from commercial, industrial, agricultural and domestic products (such as biodegradable waste that can be burnt as fuel). While biomass is renewable (and is sometimes called carbon neutral) it can still contribute to climate change: when burned as a fuel, it puts CO_2 into the atmosphere. But when biomass is used for energy production it is considered carbon neutral or a net reducer of greenhouse gases, and valuable in the waste management system because it offsets the methane that would have otherwise entered the atmosphere had it gone to landfill.

Pump It Up

Ground-source heat pumps transfer heat from the ground into a building to provide heating, and in some instances, to pre-heat domestic hot water. The heat stored in the ground is, in most cases, stored solar heat and not geothermal heat (although this will contribute in some small measure to all the heat stored in the ground). Installing a ground-source heat pump means installing lengths of pipes filled with anti-freeze and water in a borehole or horizontal trench outside your house. The system works a bit like a refrigerator, but in reverse: it extracts heat from the ground and uses it to heat your home. If it's replacing electricity, oil, LPG or coal as a heating fuel (but not gas), then there are cost savings to be had. While ground-source heat pumps can be combined with radiators, these are generally larger than with standard boiler systems so, overall, ground-source heat pumps work best with under-floor heating, as this system works at a lower temperature. There are also air-source heat pumps, which work best when the outside air temperature is relatively warm, and water-source heat pumps that can be used to provide heating for homes near rivers, streams and lakes.

A Wind Up

Wind power has been used for centuries across the world: it's free energy, efficient and produces no harmful emissions. If you are considering using renewable energy in your home then think about a domestic wind turbine. In effect, these are smaller versions of the turbines that now dot the landscape and can be fitted to houses or sited in a suitable location close to the building. To power an average-sized house fully, a domestic wind turbine needs a span of 5 m (about 16½ feet) from tip to tip, and you need good wind conditions. The average

household consumption is around 4,500 kWh, while a smaller turbine of about 2 m (6½ ft) would yield around 500 KWh a year in good conditions – this can be used to charge batteries or be sold back into the national grid. Again, there are grants available to help towards installation costs, but you can still harness the wind in a much smaller way: micro-turbines of less than 100 W can be used to charge up 12 V or 24 V batteries!

Solar Power

Harnessing the sun's power for domestic use happens in two ways: firstly, solar panels or slates can convert the energy to heat and provide hot water. These work alongside your conventional water heater and can provide up to a third of your hot water needs. The second method is by photovoltaic (PV) tiles, which can create electricity for use in the home to run lights and electrical appliances. The tiles, which cover 10–15 sq m (110–160 sq ft) of a south-east or south-west facing roof (in the northern hemisphere), are available in a variety of styles to blend in with existing roof tiles and even as transparent cells which can be used on conservatories. Solar energy is an ideal way to use a free and renewable energy and to minimize the use of other less environmentally friendly fuels, as solar systems produce no greenhouse gases.

Water

Water is a very precious resource that's vital to life, health and hygiene, but a resource that is all too often taken for granted and, more frequently, wasted. A great deal of energy is required to make mains water drinkable, to supply it to our homes, and to treat waste-water and sewerage after use. Add to that the energy needed to heat water for baths, showers, laundry and washing-up: energy means CO_2 released into the atmosphere. The good news is that when it comes to going green, simple yet highly effective changes can make a huge difference to our carbon footprints. What's more, making a few alterations to your water use will leave you with plenty of change in your pocket.

Metered Water (and Sewerage) Supplies

Unlike our other utility providers, where we can pick and switch suppliers and tariffs, most of us are stuck with the local water provider and its charges. One way in which savings can be made is to have a water meter installed. This records the amount of water used so that you pay for what you use, rather than paying a fixed amount each year based on the rateable value (RV) of your home. Even if you live alone, only take showers and never use a hosepipe, but occupy a high RV home, your annual un-metered water bill will be high, too. You can use an online price comparison site like www.uswitch.com to help you calculate your water usage and see if a water meter will save you money. Remember that, in addition to the metered water that you are charged for, you will also have to pay about the same for sewerage and waste-water provision.

Assessed Supplies

Most homes can have a water meter installed for free, but there are exceptions, such as when it's unreasonably expensive or technically impossible (in blocks of flats with shared mains supplies, for example). In these instances you can ask your water supplier to give you an assessed charge: this is where your water bill is calculated on an estimated use or is based on what other metered customers in your area pay for their water services.

Top Tips for Saving Water

 Turn off the tap: You can save 6 litres (over 12 pints) of water per minute by turning off the tap while you brush your teeth, shave, wash your hands or wash up. Get into the habit, and then try a 'California shower': get wet, turn off the shower, soap up and scrub, then rinse off!

Fix that drip: Replacing a worn washer is quick, easy and cheap. What's more, you'll stop up to 15 litres (nearly 32 pints) of water a day going down the drain: a whopping 5,500 litres (over 1,200 gallons) per year.

Don't pull for a pee: The overwhelming majority of lavatories are flushed with water that's premium quality drinking water – what a waste of a valuable and expensive resource! If you must flush, then you can reduce the volume of water by fitting a water saving device such as a 'hippo' (your water company may provide this for free, or you can fill an empty bleach bottle with sand and put it in the cistern). If you're going to upgrade your bathroom, install a low- or dual-flush. And don't forget to advertise your old bathroom suite on Freecycle – taps, pipes and all!

Don't keep the tap running: Wash your fruit and vegetables in a bowl of water; you can then use the water on the garden or for houseplants (or if you haven't pulled for a pee, put it down the lavatory!)

Save water in the garden: Get a water butt and collect rainwater for watering the borders, beds and containers. Use a watering can and not a hosepipe: but if you do need a hosepipe, fit a trigger nozzle to control the flow. You can even connect a butt up to a drainpipe to channel rainwater off the roof. If you're a mean green you would use your water butt for flushing the loo, too!

 Take a shower: You'll use about a third of the water that you would in the bath, less if you have a 'California shower' (see above). If you have a power shower, be aware that it can use more water than a bath in just five minutes, so keep an eye on the time.

 Insulate your water pipes: Put lagging around your water pipes and any outside taps to prevent burst pipes in very cold weather. Locate your main stop valve or stopcock so you know where it is in an emergency, such a burst pipe.

 Hosepipe ban: Running a hosepipe for half an hour to wash your car will use more water than the average family uses in one day! Use a bucket and a sponge instead, and rinse off using a watering can – full of water from your water butt!

Checklist

☑ **Calculate your carbon footprint:**
Consider offsetting some or all of your carbon emissions.

☑ **Switch it off completely when not in use:**
That means at the wall socket.

☑ **Don't leave electrical appliances on standby:**
They're still using power.

☑ **Switch to energy-efficient light bulbs:**
And turn the lights out when you leave a room empty –
even low-energy bulbs still use energy.

☑ **Insulate and draught-proof your home:**
This keeps the heat in and the cold out.

☑ **Turn your central heating down by just 1° C:**
This will save money and energy.

☑ **Consider switching to a greener alternative:**
Change energy tariffs, and give serious thought to wind or solar power.

☑ **Don't waste water:** It is a precious resource.

Cleaning

Cleaning Products

Supermarket shelves are positively groaning under the weight of cleaning products for floors, ovens, sinks, tiles, lavatories and bathrooms as well as for laundry. Manufacturers would have us believe that they are both essential and super-efficient for keeping our homes clean. In reality, the vast majority are not really needed and, what's more, their manufacture and use can be devastating to the environment. There are greener alternatives: brands such as Ecover and Method are widely available, and there are lots of household products already in your cupboards that will do the cleaning just as well, so long as you are prepared to add a little elbow grease.

It's Natural But...

Just because something is natural doesn't mean it's harmless: cyanide, mercury, arsenic and uranium are all natural substances but you wouldn't want them in your home! When it comes to the vast majority of commercially produced cleaning products, all of them (even the bar of soap for washing your hands) contain harmful chemicals that will end up going down the drain and into our rivers, lakes and oceans.

What's In It?

We all use ordinary soap on a daily basis and think nothing of it, but millions of tonnes of soap go down the drain every year, causing a serious environmental impact and an additional strain on marine life. Most soaps contain a bewildering array of chemicals and synthetic fragrances. MIT (methylisothiazolinone) and Triclosan (which the Environmental Protection Agency classifies as a pesticide) are both chemicals found in anti-bacterial soaps, hand and body washes. Once these substances go down the plug and into the water system, they carry on killing bacteria, both good and bad. Although hospitals and health centres may need such soaps,

according to the Center for Disease Control in Atlanta, Georgia, USA, washing with normal soap is enough for ordinary use, as it dislodges bacteria that is then rinsed away with water.

Greener Alternatives

Vegetable soaps, such as olive oil soap, are made with plant oils and use natural fragrances like lavender and glycerine. No animal fats (tallow) are used in making them, so they are good for vegans and vegetarians and kinder to the environment.

Castile Soap

Green websites and retailers sell this type of soap. Castile is not a brand name but refers to a type of soap. Castile soap, also known as seafarer's soap, is made exclusively from vegetable oils (no animal fats) and contains no synthetic substances. Olive oil is the main vegetable oil used in the best castile soaps, but there are variations that use coconut and jojoba oils. If soap is advertised or labelled as castile, you can be sure that it's a fairly green product.

Green Cautions and Precautions

When it comes to cleaning, going green makes sense, and the alternatives suggested in this chapter are less toxic and environmentally damaging than commonly sold commercial cleaning products. Nevertheless, it's important to take some precautions:

 Wear gloves: Especially if you have sensitive skin.

 Spot test: Do a spot test of your green cleaner on a hidden area before applying it to the entire surface.

 Handle with care: Essential oils in their pure form can be corrosive and highly toxic. Hydrogen peroxide and borax are extremely useful and versatile cleaning substances but should still be handled with care and stored out of reach of children.

The Greener Cleaners

There is no need to buy a different cleaner for every purpose – all you need is a basic cleaning kit consisting of a green washing-up liquid. To this you will need to add some items from your kitchen cupboards:

 Bicarbonate of soda (baking soda or sodium bicarbonate).

 Vinegar.

 Lemons.

 Salt.

From the pharmacist, you can easily purchase:

 Hydrogen peroxide.
 Eucalyptus oil.

And from the hardware store:

 Borax.

Reduce, Recycle, Reuse

The environmental mantra 'reduce, recycle, reuse' can also be applied to green cleaning.

Recycling Ideas

Try these green cleaning recycling ideas:

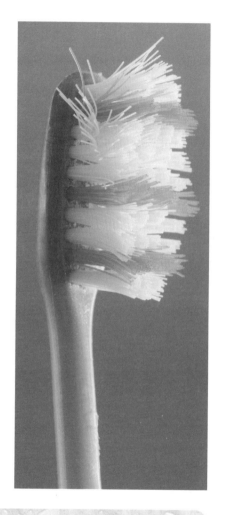

- **Water**: Reuse washing-up water by putting it down the lavatory or in the garden.
- **Clothes**: Keep old, worn-out T-shirts and turn them into dusters and cleaning cloths.
- **Toothbrushes**: Keep your old tooth- and nailbrushes; these make great scrubbing brushes for hard-to-reach nooks and crannies.

Have You Thought Of?

If you're right-handed, then this glove will wear out first. Don't throw away the leftover left-handed glove, turn it inside out and use it on your right hand!

Brilliant Bicarb

Bicarbonate of soda, also known as sodium bicarbonate and baking soda (but not *baking powder*, which is the raising agent used in cakes), is made from refined soda ash that is derived in one of two ways, both of which have environmental impacts. The first method starts with mining trona ore (the world's largest deposits of which are found in the Green River Basin in Wyoming, USA), which is extracted by underground room-and-pillar mining and then refined. The second is the Solvay method, in which carbon dioxide and ammonia are injected into a concentrated solution of sodium chloride. A by-product of the latter method is calcium chloride in a liquid solution; when discharged into waterways, this can increase salinity. Nevertheless, bicarb is a cheap and extremely versatile cleaning agent that is still a green substitute for many harsher chemicals.

Around the House with Bicarb

Bicarbonate of soda has many uses: it's a great deodorizer, a desiccant (i.e. it can be used as a drying agent), a stain remover and a de-greaser. There are also a number of uses for bicarb for personal use, for brushing teeth (see Fashion & Beauty page 154 and in the garden. Bicarbonate of soda is also a fire retardant: when it burns, it produces carbon dioxide and starves the flames of oxygen, so keep a pot by your stove/hob (remember to turn the gas supply off if you do have a fire), by your open fire or garden incinerator and throw it on to extinguish flames.

As a Deodorizer

 Fridge: An eggcup of bicarbonate of soda placed on a shelf or in the fridge door will soak up odours and absorb excess moisture.

- **Bins**: Sprinkle in the base of kitchen waste bins and outside trash cans to stop them smelling.
- **Shoes**: Fill the toes of old socks or tights with bicarb, tie a knot in the end and place in smelly trainers, shoes and boots.
- **Kitty litter**: Sprinkled and mixed into kitty litter, bicarb will help keep the odours down.
- **Animal (and human) urine spills**: Sprinkle with plenty of bicarb to absorb moisture and smells. Let it dry then sweep or vacuum up.
- **Mops**: Deodorize mops by soaking them in a bucket of water with 4 tbsp of bicarb.
- **Carpet**: Most carpet deodorizing powders are bicarb-based, so save money and sprinkle your carpets with neat bicarb and then vacuum. You can even sprinkle some bicarb in the vacuum cleaner bag to keep that odour-free as well.

As a Desiccant

- **Grease and oil**: Sprinkle liberally on fresh grease and oil spills to draw up the oil, then scrape up and dispose of.
- **Soak up excess moisture**: Sprinkled into drawers or placed in a bowl in closed areas like wardrobes, bicarb will help control humidity. Stir it up occasionally for maximum effect. Alternatively, tie up some sticks of school chalk with a piece of pretty ribbon and place in a drawer or closet to absorb any moisture.

As a Stain Remover

- **Porcelain and plastic**: Stains on porcelain (such as cups, sinks and toilets) and plastic can often be shifted by applying a layer of bicarbonate of soda and working it with a damp sponge.
- **Collars and cuffs**: A paste of bicarb and water worked into the collars and cuffs of shirts (use an old toothbrush or nailbrush) prior to washing will remove stubborn stains.
- **Wood**: Water stains on wooden surfaces can be lifted with a damp sponge dipped in a solution of bicarb and water. Be careful not to soak the wood too much or you'll raise and swell the grain of the wood.
- **Wallpaper**: Crayon marks on walls come off if you apply a paste of bicarb and water with an old soft toothbrush and lightly brush the area.

As a General Cleaner

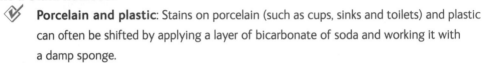

- **Chrome**: A bicarb and water paste makes a terrific chrome cleaner. Let the paste dry then buff with a soft cloth.
- **Rust**: A paste of bicarb and vinegar applied with a pot scourer will remove light rust.
- **Microwaves**: Steam-clean microwaves and banish lingering food smells by dissolving 2 tbsp of bicarb in water in a (microwave-safe) bowl, then set the microwave on high for a minute or two.
- **Fruit and veg**: Chemical and pesticide residues can be washed off fruit and vegetables in a large bowl of water with 3 tbsp of bicarb added.
- **Fridges and freezers**: Sprinkle bicarb on a damp sponge to clean fridges and freezers after defrosting. It will also clean china, stainless steel and kitchen worktops without scratching them.
- **Pots and pans**: Rescue scorched pans by removing as much burned-on food from the bottom as possible, then cover the bottom with a good layer of bicarb, add a little water and let the pan soak overnight. Scrape off in the morning with a wooden or plastic utensil.

Versatile Vinegar

Vinegar has been in use around the world for more than 5,000 years as a condiment and for its medicinal properties. Although 'vinegar' means 'spur wine', not all are made from the grape: brown malt vinegar (popular on fish and chips in the UK) is made from barley; white vinegar (used primarily for pickling) is made from maize. There are also rice vinegars, cider-apple vinegar, cane-sugar and corn-sugar vinegars, coconut-, plum-, date- and raisin-derived vinegars, as well as red and white wine vinegar (including sherry and Champagne versions) and the famous balsamic vinegar, which is a speciality of Modena in Italy.

Vinegar's Cleaning Properties

Vinegar is one of the best green cleaners. With acidity levels typically between four and eight per cent by volume for condiment (table) vinegar, it's acidic enough to dissolve the alkalis in soaps without harming fabrics. White vinegar, at five per cent acidity by volume, used neat (undiluted) for cleaning is effective against *E.Coli*, *Salmonella* and *Staphyloccus*, so make it part of your green cleaning routine.

Vinegar for Stains and Odour Removal

- **Pre-wash**: A spray bottle with a 50-50 dilution of white vinegar and water makes a handy pre-wash stain remover. Treat underarms, cuffs and collars with a spray before laundering.
- **Grease stains**: These can be treated before laundering, using a paste of two parts white vinegar and three parts bicarbonate of soda (baking soda). Apply to the garment with an old toothbrush or soft nailbrush and gently brush into the fabric. Let the paste set for half an hour before laundering. This also works for mildew spots.

Old, set stains: These can be treated using a solution of 3 tbsp of white vinegar, 2 tbsp of green dishwashing liquid and 1 litre/2 pints/4½ cups of warm water. Sponge and blot the stain repeatedly and then launder.

Bloodstains: These are easy to remove *before* they dry but can be hard to shift once set into a fabric. Pour undiluted white vinegar onto fresh bloodstains and let it soak for 10–15 minutes. Blot with a clean cloth and repeat if necessary, and then launder as usual.

Ink stains: Vinegar cuts through grease and oil and the main carrier of ball point and roller ball inks is castor oil, so vinegar can be used to remove these marks. Blot first with undiluted white vinegar, then gently rub in a paste of two parts vinegar and three parts cornflour. Let the paste dry, brush off excess and launder.

Bright whites: White garments or fabrics that have yellowed can be made bright again by an overnight soak in a solution of 12 parts warm water and one part white vinegar. Delicate or antique lace can also be restored, but use a more diluted solution: 24 parts water to one part white vinegar, and rinse well.

Deodorizer: You can deodorize clothes without resorting to chemical dry cleaning. Put 145 ml/5 fl oz/²⁄₃ cup of white vinegar into the bathtub and pour in a kettleful of hot water. Hang the smelly garments in the bathroom, close the door and let the vinegar steam deodorize them. Hang garments in an open space to dry out afterwards.

Fabric Conditioner and Colour Fix

The acidic nature of white vinegar cuts through grease and neutralizes the alkalis that form the base of many soaps and detergents, making it an effective fabric softener and clothes conditioner.

Fabric softener: Revive and make cotton and wool blankets soft and fluffy by adding 230 ml/8 fl oz/1 cup of white vinegar to the wash's final rinse cycle.

Colour fixer: Fix the colour in garments before their first wash by soaking them for a few minutes in a bowl of diluted white vinegar.

Bleaching agent: Say goodbye to chlorine bleach; white vinegar in the rinse cycle is just as effective as a bleaching agent, and it deodorizes and softens at the same time. What's more, it's greener than chlorine bleach and has no harmful fumes.

Neutralizer: White vinegar breaks down uric acid so is good for rinsing baby and children's clothes and underwear, and for rinsing terry diapers. It neutralizes the alkalis in soaps and balances the pH level, helping to avoid diaper rash.

Cleaner and Descaler

Washing machine and dishwasher: Clean these once in a while by pouring in about 230 ml/8 fl oz/1 cup of white vinegar and running the machine on full cycle (but without clothes or dishes and using no detergent). The vinegar will clean out any residual soap scum, remove mineral deposits and deodorize the machines.

Kettles and coffee makers: Limescale and mineral deposits that have built up in kettles and coffee makers can be removed by brewing up enough white vinegar to fill the pot three-quarters full and then leaving overnight. Rinse out with cold water.

Iron: De-fur a steam iron by partly filling with white vinegar, turning it on and leaving it to steam away the vinegar. Repeat with clean water.

Sinks, basins, showers and bathtubs: To un-clog plug holes, pour 4–5 tbsp of bicarbonate of soda down the plug hole then pour in 120 ml/4 fl oz/$\frac{1}{2}$ cup of white vinegar. The mix will fizz and foam; when it stops, flush through with very hot water. Wait five minutes, then flush with cold water. As well as clearing any blockages, you will also remove odour-creating bacteria that were lurking there.

Lavatory bowl: Disinfect and clean your lavatory bowl without harmful chemicals. 500 ml/1 pint/$2\frac{1}{2}$ cups of neat white vinegar poured around the sides of the bowl last thing at night on a weekly basis will also keep any tide marks at bay.

Windows: Vinegar makes a great window cleaner – it removes grease, grime and rain water marks as well as keeping flies away. Wash the windows in a 50-50 solution of water and vinegar, then polish dry with scrunched-up newspaper or brown paper for a streak-free, sparkling finish.

Anti-Bacterial Cleaner

✔ **Laundry**: The acetic acid content of white vinegar makes it anti-bacterial. 120 ml/ 4 fl oz/½ cup of white vinegar added to the rinse cycle of a wash, especially if it contains terry diapers, sports socks and jocks, and towels, will kill any bacteria in the load.

✔ **Cutting boards and counter tops**: White vinegar is effective against *E.Coli*, *Salmonella* and *Staphyloccus*, so use it neat to clean down wooden and plastic cutting boards, butcher's blocks and non-marble counter tops before and after food preparation.

✔ **Fridge**: Equal parts of white vinegar and water make an effective fridge cleaner, both for inside and out. Mould or mildew in nooks and crannies can be treated with neat white vinegar.

✔ **Kitchen de-greaser**: A cloth dampened with a 50-50 diluted mix of water and white vinegar makes an effective kitchen de-greaser.

✔ **Cloudy glasses**: These can be made clear again if you soak them for 10–15 minutes in a 50-50 solution of white vinegar and warm water. Scrub gently with a soft bottle brush and rinse off.

✔ **Plastic food containers and vacuum flasks**: These can get stained and scented by strong foods and liquids. Wash them in a solution of equal parts white vinegar and water then rinse clean. Store them with their lids off. For persistent odours, soak a slice of bread in vinegar and pop that into the container with the lid on. Leave it overnight, then rinse out.

✔ **Loofahs and natural sponges**: Soak these in vinegar to rid them of soap residues. Rinse off, then soak them in a brine bath to remove any slime before a final rinse in cold water.

Mildew and Mould

✔ **Grout between tiles**: This is a breeding ground for bacteria; scrub the grout with an old toothbrush or nailbrush dipped into neat white vinegar.

✔ **Closets and chests**: Musty smelling closets and chests need cleaning and airing unless you want clothes and linens stored in them to smell too. Mix a solution of

120 ml/4 fl oz/$\frac{1}{2}$ cup white vinegar, 120 ml/4 fl oz/$\frac{1}{2}$ cup ammonia, 4 tbsp bicarbonate of soda in a bucket with 4 litres/1 gallon of water. Wash all the surfaces and let them dry out before returning items to storage.

Shower curtains: Wash mildew- or mould-stained shower curtains in equal parts of laundry detergent (green of course!) and bicarbonate of soda, then rinse with 120 ml/4 fl oz/$\frac{1}{2}$ cup of white vinegar added to the rinse water. Hang the curtain back up and let it air-dry.

Other Natural Cleaning Products

If you decide to go green in the house, you are doing yourself and the environment a huge favour: you won't come into contact with toxic chemicals and noxious fumes on a daily basis, and you will help reduce the amount of chemical residues that leach into water courses and land. You'll save money in the long term, too: most of the products listed in this chapter cost very little. Here are some more natural cleaning products that are kind to the planet and will leave your home spick and span.

Salt and Lemons

As well as being two of the three vital ingredients in a Tequila Slammer, salt and lemons have for centuries been used as household cleaners. Individually they are very useful: lemons are acidic (like white vinegar, about five per cent by volume), and anti-bacterial; and the granular nature of salt makes it ideal as a scourer. Together they make an extremely effective, very green team.

Cleaning with Salt and Lemons

- **Mud stains**: Sprinkle salt liberally on mud stains, let it soak up the moisture then brush or vacuum off.
- **Soot falls from open fires**: This can make a real mess! Sprinkle salt onto soot to absorb the grease and then vacuum or sweep up. Then get your chimney professionally cleaned.
- **Food spills on hobs and in ovens**: These are harder to remove if they get baked on. Keep a pot of salt handy to cover new spills, then wipe off when the hob or oven has cooled.

Copper pans: Rub salt and lemon juice over the copper bottoms of pans to restore the shine. Do note, however, that the duller the copper, the better it conducts the heat, making it more energy efficient.

Aluminium and stainless steel pans: When these become discoloured they can be revived by boiling some water and lemon juice in them.

Wooden chopping boards: Scour these with a sprinkling of salt and rub with the cut side of half a lemon.

Iron: Keep the sole plate of your iron clean and remove any sticky patches by passing it backwards and forwards over a sheet of paper sprinkled with salt.

Tea and coffee cups: Stained cups can be cleaned by gently rubbing a paste of salt and lemon on them and rinsing afterwards.

Windscreens: A small fabric bag filled with salt, slightly moistened and rubbed across a car windscreen will stop ice forming on it.

Room freshener: A 50-50 solution of water and lemon juice in a spray diffuser makes a great room freshener.

Sink and taps: Clean limescale from a sink or around taps (faucets) by rubbing with half a lemon.

Trash cans: Deodorize your garbage disposal unit by feeding a sliced-up lemon through it.

Washing-up: A teaspoon of lemon juice added to the washing-up water can help cut through grease.

Drains: Hot lemon juice and bicarbonate of soda makes a great drain cleaner, and one that's safe to use in septic systems.

Borax

Borax is basically a naturally occurring salt and is also known as sodium borate or sodium tetraborate. It is mined at Boron, Arizona, USA, as well as in Turkey, Chile and Tibet, and is used in a whole range of products including cosmetics, pesticides, insecticides, insulation materials (it's also a flame retardant) and cleaners. You can buy it at hardware stores: just ask for borax or one of the most popular brands like Dri-Pak (UK) or 20 Mule Team (North America). Even though it's natural and a greener alternative to many detergents, it's still sensible to handle borax with care as it can cause skin irritation in some people.

Cleaning With Borax

 Laundry: 50 g/2 oz/¹/₂ cup of borax added to the wash will rid clothes and bedding of urine smells and stains.

 Toilet: 25g/1 oz/¹/₄ cup of borax put in the lavatory bowl, allowed to sit for a while and then brushed around the sides before flushing will clean and deodorize the toilet. It will also do the same to your toilet brush.

Have You Thought Of?

Sprinkling borax onto your carpet to kill fleas?
Leave it overnight, then vacuum it up.

- **Pre-soak**: You can use borax as a pre-soaker for laundry. Add 1 tbsp of borax to each 4 litres/1 gallon of water and let the garments soak for 30 minutes.
- **Colour enhancer**: Borax is safe to use on coloured garments. 50 g/2 oz/^{1}/$_2$ cup added to the wash will boost the detergent's cleaning power and make coloured garments brighter.
- **Tile cleaner**: A mix of 1 tsp eco dishwashing liquid, 1 tsp of borax and 1 litre/2 pints of warm water in a spray bottle makes a great tile cleaner for kitchens and bathrooms. Spray on, let it rest, rinse off and air-dry.

Hydrogen Peroxide

Hydrogen peroxide will be familiar to anyone who's ever gone blonde. It's a greener alternative to household chlorine bleach (sodium hypochlorite), which forms more toxic by-products, such as dioxins, furans and other organochlorines, when it reacts with other chemicals. Produced by both plant and animal cells, hydrogen peroxide occurs naturally in the environment by sunlight acting on water. Hydrogen peroxide is simply water with an extra oxygen molecule (H202) and it breaks down into oxygen and water. Peroxide is readily from chemist's shops, pharmacists and drug stores and is available in solutions of two and three per cent.

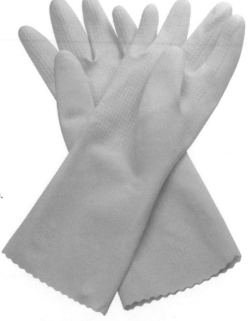

Hydrogen Peroxide Tips

- **Keep out of direct sunlight**: Otherwise you'll end up with oxygen and water! Store it in a dark bottle, well out reach of children.
- **Wear gloves**: It's a bleach. Get your finger ends in it and you'll see they turn white; don't be alarmed, this is not harmful, and it's great for getting stained fingers clean.

Cleaning with Hydrogen Peroxide

- **Anti-bacterial**: A three per cent solution of hydrogen peroxide dabbed on a clean cloth can be used to clean food preparation countertops, cutting boards and surfaces. It will kill *Salmonella* and other bacteria.
- **Disinfectant**: Half-fill a spray bottle with three per cent hydrogen peroxide and top up with water; you can use the spray as a lavatory and bathroom disinfectant.
- **Treat mould**: Spray on solution made with one part hydrogen peroxide and two parts water – a handy treatment for mould on bathroom tiles
- **Bleaching agent**: Hydrogen peroxide is a greener alternative to chlorine bleach. 230 ml/8 fl oz/1 cup of three per cent hydrogen peroxide added to your wash load will keep your whites white.
- **Remove limescale**: A paste of three per cent hydrogen peroxide and bicarbonate of soda applied to taps (faucets) removes stubborn water stains and limescale.
- **Toothbrushes**: These can be disinfected by dipping in hydrogen peroxide, followed by a rinse off in clean water. This is useful if your bathroom houses the lavatory – every time you flush, faecal spores can be spread through the air! Even better, put the lid down before you flush!
- **Mirrors and glass**: Use hydrogen peroxide for cleaning mirrors and glass. Don't spray on but wipe on with a cloth or a coffee filter and wipe off with a lint-free cloth.
- **Sterilizer**: Hydrogen peroxide can be used to sterilize cuts and abrasions, but it'll sting. The fizzing that occurs is normal. Rinse off with clean water afterwards.

Eucalyptus Oil

The eucalyptus or gum tree is the main genus of trees in Australia: there are over 600 species and they account for some 75 per cent of the continent's flora. In Australia, eucalyptus has provided timber for building, fuel, and wood pulp for paper making, as well as being a source of nectar for honeybees. One of the most widely used by-products is eucalyptus oil, with its distinctive scent. Some eucalyptus oils are mixed with camphor extract, but if you want 100 per cent pure Australian eucalyptus oil then read the labels carefully – look for brands such as FGB Natural Products and Emu Ridge. As well as its medicinal uses, eucalyptus oil can also be used around the house, replacing many harsh, synthetic and environmentally unfriendly products.

Cleaning with Eucalyptus Oil

- **Get rid of sticky marks**: Fill a spray bottle nearly full of water, add a capful of 100 per cent eucalyptus oil and a squeeze of eco-friendly washing up liquid. Shake it up to mix, spray on and wipe off: it gets rid of sticky marks and fingerprints on laminated surfaces.

- **Disinfectant**: Pour 50 ml/1.5 fl oz of eucalyptus oil into 1 litre/2 pints/4 ½ cups water; decant into a clean bottle. Store this and use it as you would any commercial disinfectant.

- **Laundry**: The disinfectant and anti-microbial properties of eucalyptus oil are useful in the laundry, so add 1 tsp to the washing load.

- **Deodorizer**: The great scent of eucalyptus oil makes it a wonderful deodorizer. Revive those cardboard tree-shaped deodorizers that hang in cars with a drop of eucalyptus oil.

- **Get rid of creepy crawlies**: It seems spiders don't like eucalyptus. If you don't like them, a drop on a cotton wool ball placed under the bed, in closets/cupboards or in dark corners will send them packing.

- **Lavatory cleaner**: A really effective and green lavatory cleaner can be made if you fill a leftover squeezy bottle three-quarters full of white vinegar and add the juice of one lemon and 1 tsp of eucalyptus oil. The squeezy bottle lets you aim right under the rim!

- **Remove oil and tar**: Nothing works better than eucalyptus oil for removing oil or tar from skin, both human and pet. Dab it on with a clean rag to remove sticky deposits gently from feet, hands and paws.

Checklist

- **Handle with care**: Even though they are green, take care when handling all cleaning products; wear rubber gloves and wash your hands afterwards, too.

- **Spot test**: Do a spot test of your green cleaner on a hidden area before applying it to the entire surface.

- **Replace cleaning essentials with green alternatives**: In most homes, the cleaning *essentials* really consist of dish-washing liquid, laundry detergent, disinfectant, a scourer and bleach. Eco-friendly varieties of all of these are available.

- **Bicarbonate of soda**: This has many uses – it's a great deodorizer, a desiccant, a stain remover and a de-greaser.

- **Vinegar**: This is one of the best green cleaners. Use it for stain and odour removal, as a descaler, as an anti-bacterial cleaner and to get rid of mildew and mould.

- **Lemons and salt**: Lemons are acidic and anti-bacterial and the granular nature of salt makes it ideal as a scourer.

- **Use hydrogen peroxide, eucalyptus oil and borax**: These can all be used to clean the home in an environmentally friendly way.

- **Reuse and recycle**: Old T-shirts and tooth- and nailbrushes can be reused as cleaning implements.

Garden

Green Fingers

No matter where you live, there's always room for some plants: flowers grown in pots, tubs and containers, herbs on a windowsill, tomatoes in hanging baskets, or even potatoes in wheelie bins. Big or small, growing your own produce is a great way to make sure you are getting the very best without adding chemical pesticides to your body and to the earth. And with the ever-expanding range of heritage and heirloom seeds available, you'll not only get tastier produce, you'll also be helping to maintain the genetic biodiversity that is threatened by increasingly commercial agriculture.

Plants and Flowers

You don't have to become completely self-sufficient; you can be green in your garden, window box or container garden. Don't think you have to produce only edible produce as all plants have a vital role to play in our environment. Brightly coloured or sweetly scented flowers attract insects vital for pollination, and berry-bearing shrubs and bushes offer food and habitats for birds and wildlife.

The Ground Beneath Your Feet

Some plants like the air around them sunny and dry, others like it shady and moist. The same is true of where plants put their feet: some want their soil acid, others want it alkaline. You can find out if your soil is acid or alkaline by doing a simple test, for which you'll need those eco-friendly all-rounders vinegar and bicarbonate of soda.

To Test for Acid Soil:

Mix a handful of your garden soil with 120 ml/4 fl oz/½ cup of water and 2 heaped tbsp of bicarbonate of soda. If the soil fizzes and bubbles, then it's acid soil.

To Test for Alkaline Soil:

Mix a handful of soil with 120 ml/4 fl oz/¹⁄₂ cup of white vinegar in a jar. If the soil bubbles and fizzes, your soil is alkaline.

Large Garden

If you have a large garden, repeat the tests at various points around it to see if it's acid or alkaline throughout. To find the exact pH levels, you'll need a simple testing kit, which you can get from a garden centre or hardware store.

Increase Soil Acidity

Some plants, such as azaleas, rhododendrons and hydrangeas, thrive in more acid soils. Yellowing on the plants' leaves can indicate that there's been a shift in the soil's pH level, or that there's a lack of iron. If you live in a hard water area, the acidity levels in your area might also be low. You can increase the soil's acidity by adding 240 ml/8 fl oz/1 cup of white vinegar to a large bucket of water and watering once a week for three weeks. The vinegar raises the level of acidity but also works to release iron in the soil for the plants' use.

Increase Soil Alkalinity

Flower species that prefer alkaline soil include geraniums, begonias and hydrangeas. To raise potting soil alkalinity, apply some baking soda. However, use it sparingly; correction of overly acidic soil should be considered a long-term project. It is better to test your soil each year and make your adjustments gradually. The addition of hardwood ash, bone meal, crushed marble or crushed oyster shells will also help to raise the soil's pH.

Grow Your Own Food

Growing your own food will not only give you low-cost organic produce, but you'll also get hours of pleasure and a great sense of achievement. The best way forward is to start simply; once you become more experienced and confident, you can then move on to growing greater varieties. You don't need a big space to grow – plants will live happily in pots and containers but you must water and feed them in order to get the best crop. If your garden is paved over, you could lift some paving stones and plant into the ground, or construct some raised beds instead. With clever forward planning, raised beds let you grow crop after crop in quite a small space.

Little Green Fingers

A sure way of getting children to eat their greens is to get them involved in growing them! Most children love looking after their own plot and it gives them an opportunity to learn more about their food and about nature in general. You can now buy child-friendly gardening tools that make handling easier. There are lots of easy-to-grow vegetables and fruit: cherry tomatoes can be grown in hanging baskets and blueberries (such as the variety Top Hat) can be grown in containers. Encourage children to plant fun things like sunflowers (and have a 'who can grow the biggest' competition) and herbs like lavender, thyme and sage to attract wildlife.

What to Grow

Growing your own fruit and vegetables can be a process of trial and error; the more you do, the more you learn which crops suit your soil, the aspect (sunny or partial shade, windy or still) and climate. Some crops may need extra care, while others grow happily without much intervention. For the most part, green gardeners want to produce a variety of fruit and

vegetables throughout the year, so you'll need to plan a vegetable calendar plotting sowing, growing and harvesting times in order to make use of your available space and the growing season. Keep a record of what's grown where so you can rotate your crops. There are many useful websites offering gardening tips and techniques.

Cabbage Patch

Brassicas, the cabbage family, are the stars in the spring and autumn vegetable garden and include the different cabbages (pointed and round), broccoli, kale, Brussels sprouts and cauliflowers. In the kitchen pharmacy, brassicas are valued for their nutritional value: they provide large amounts of vitamin C and soluble fibre and contain nutrients with potent anti-cancer properties. Brassicas are greedy vegetables to grow (especially cauliflowers) and like well-drained soil that is rich in organic matter, but the range of varieties is enormous. You can even grow different coloured ones: Violet Queen and Cheddar cauliflowers are purple and orange respectively and cabbages can also be either green or red, so you can add great splashes of colour to your garden.

Back To Your Roots

Sweet and nutritious root vegetables like radishes, beetroots, carrots, onions, garlic, turnips and swedes are very easy to grow. They are cold-weather crops that mature in the spring or autumn, and are seeded directly into well-drained loose ground, as they don't like being transplanted. Don't forget that the leafy tops of root vegetables, especially beetroots, can be eaten like salad leaves. Furthermore, root vegetables are power houses of health, full of vitamins and minerals vital to see the body through the long, dark winter months.

Luscious Legumes

The huge *Fabaceae* family (once known as *Leguminosae*, legumes) contains over 16,000 varieties so you can guarantee that there will be one you can grow successfully on your plot! Common edible legumes include peas, broad beans, string beans, French beans and runner beans. Gardeners in the northern hemisphere are keen to plant peas as soon as winter is over, and they are usually among the first crops planted in spring gardens.

Salad Days

Summer wouldn't be the same without salads, but if you're fortunate enough to have a greenhouse or even a garden frame, you can grow crisp lettuces and other salad crops such as rocket (arugula), mizuna and spring onions (scallions) over a much longer period. Most salad crops should be sown a few seeds at a time every two weeks rather than all at once: this gives you a continuous crop. Many salad crops can also be grown as 'cut and come again', whereby you take a few leaves from the plant on a regular basis, allowing new leaves to grow back. Another advantage to growing salad crops is that while they can also be planted and grown in the soil, they can be grown easily in containers. These can be 23–25 cm (9–10 in) pots or growing bags but remember that extra care needs to be taken over feeding and watering, as the small volume of compost soon gets dried out and exhausted. Pots and growing bags are also ideal for aubergines (eggplants), cucumbers, peppers (including chillies) and tomatoes. Growing crops in growing bags is a space-saving way to have a supply of fresh, organic vegetables and you can move them around into the sunniest parts of your space.

Tutti Frutti

You don't need an orchard to enjoy home-grown fruit; there are many varieties of apple and pear trees that are well suited to small-space gardening and some that can be grown as espaliers, trained along south-facing walls or fences. There are also many soft fruits that now have thornless varieties and others, like strawberries and blueberries, that make good plants for containers – so you get a good crop, whatever the size of your garden. Blueberries like acid soil, so grow them in a container with ericaceous compost and mulch with pine needles. Strawberries take up very little room and produce gorgeous flowers and tasty fruits. They can be grown in a container or in hanging baskets, well out of reach of slugs. Five or six plants will fit neatly into a good-sized basket. Water every day during the growing season and from flowering to harvest, and feed them every ten days with a high potassium feed (tomato feed works well). If you're lucky, the same plants will produce fruits the following year, but you will get a better crop if the plants are renewed.

Have You Thought Of?
Saving rain and grey water for use in the garden?

King Of The Crop

No vegetable patch would be complete without the potato. There are three main types of potato: first earlies (ready to lift in June), second earlies (ready in July and August) and maincrops (ready from late August through to October depending on when they are planted and harvested). Grow a selection of all three and have glorious potatoes practically all year round, as you can store maincrops over winter. You don't even need to have a garden because you can grow them in large containers or even in black bin liners. Some gardeners even use old car tyres stacked on top of each other. Line the bottom of the container with 15 cm (6 in) of compost and plant the seed tuber just below this. As the new stem grows, keep adding compost until the container is full. You have to keep earthing up the developing potatoes to stop the light from turning them green (green potatoes are poisonous). Keep the crops well watered in dry weather: the important time is once the tubers start to develop, and a liquid feed of balanced general fertilizer every two weeks can increase yields.

Fertilizers: Green or Not?

While it's true that your soil or plants won't be able to tell the difference between organic fertilizer and synthetic (chemical) ones, the differences in the impact that organic fertilizers make to the earth's ecosystems are significant. So, what's the difference? Synthetic fertilizers are a cocktail of chemicals engineered to mimic the naturally occurring nutrients in humus.

Synthetic Versus Organic

There are a number of problems with synthetic fertilizers. And, on the other hand, there are many advantages to using organic fertilizers.

Problems With Synthetic Fertilizers

- **Chemicals are absorbed into the crops**: And then into animals and humans, with possible long-term side effects.
- **Require special handling**: Since they are chemicals, safety gloves, overalls, boots, goggles, facemasks and breathing filters should be worn when handling.
- **Can devastate the natural soil structure.**
- **Can encourage weed growth**: They are fast-release improvers of the soil, and rich soil encourages weed growth, which then means dosing everything with pesticides to reduce the weeds.
- **Can lead to over-farming**: They work quickly and effectively, encouraging widespread use of the land, which can lead to over-farming, burnt-out roots in crops and sterile, contaminated land.
- **Can end up in water supplies**: The inorganic and toxic compounds that get washed out of the soil by rain can end up in the wrong place, such as drinking water supplies.

Advantages of Organic Fertilizers

- **Slow release**: This means you don't get over-fertilization of the soil or root damage problems.
- **Slow working**: Organic fertilizers improve the condition of the soil over the growing season.
- **Good at maintaining organic soil structure**: And also allow naturally occurring bacteria, fungi and micro-organisms to carry on living.
- **No nasties**: Won't introduce toxic chemicals into the soil or water systems.
- **Encourage wildlife**: Encourage higher and healthier populations of birds, butterflies, bees and other pollinating insects, river and lake fish, and the mammals that feed on them, as well as wild flowers.

Why Do We Need Fertilizers?

Soil gives its energy and nutrients to the plants it supports, so these have to be replaced over time.

Nitrogen, Potash and Phosphates

Fertilizers are mixtures of three things that are all found in healthy soil: nitrogen, potash and phosphates. Depending on the type of soil in your garden or allotment, there may be more or less of one ingredient, and some types of plants need more of one and perhaps less of another. For example:

- **Nitrogen-needy plants**: These are the leafy green ones, like lettuce, cabbages, Brussels sprouts, celery, leeks and spinach.
- **Phosphate-lovers**: These are root and tuberous plants, such as carrots and potatoes.
- **Potash**: This is needed by fruit, like tomatoes, and flowers.

What Makes an Organic Fertilizer?

Rather than being based on the water-soluble ammonium salts that are the main ingredient of chemical fertilizers, organic fertilizers are composed only of natural organic waste.

Examples of Organic Fertilizers

- **Humus**: Decayed kitchen and garden waste that has been turned into compost (see later in the chapter for more on composting at home).
- **Bone meal**: Crushed and ground animal bones are used to provide phosphorus.
- **Fish, blood and bone**: Derived from rendered surplus animal material, it has a balance of all three major plant nutrients – nitrogen, potassium and phosphorus.
- **Seaweed**: Kelp and bladderwrack contain all the major soil nutrients, as well as a full range of trace elements. Seaweed breaks down quickly and helps bind the soil together. You can gather it fresh from the sea or buy it in dried meal form or as concentrated liquid feed for leaf feed or root-zone feeding.
- **Fish emulsion**: A waste product from fish processing. It provides nitrogen and sulphur, but also has traces of phosphorus and potassium as well as other trace elements.

Caution

Always read the label before using any type of fertilizer, wear a face mask and gloves and ensure you wash your hands afterwards.

A Crock of Manure

Nitrogen-rich animal manure (or dung) has been used for thousands of years as a fertilizer for farming. Most farms and stables will usually have a good supply of horse or cow manure that they'd be happy to get rid of, but if it's free, it's probably very fresh and you'll have to compost it on your own premises for about eight weeks. If it's for sale, the chances are it's older and closer to being usable. If you can, go for manure from a certified organic farm. The downside to manure is that it will inevitably contain undigested seeds, so when you muck spread, you may find some unexpected plants among your crops.

Good Dung

There are a number of types of manure to choose from but remember that they all vary in their nutrient content.

- **Sheep manure**: This is a fine and gentle soil improver. It doesn't contain many nutrients but, because it is partly decayed vegetable matter, it can be dug easily into the soil.
- **Well-rotted cow manure**: This has a low nitrogen content so can be spread liberally into the soil to improve structure.
- **Poultry manure**: This is a good source of nitrogen but too strong to dig directly into the soil as it will burn plants. It needs to be well composted with lots of organic matter for about eight weeks before adding to the soil.
- **Horse manure**: The salts in the urine contained in the straw and manure will burn plants if dug into or spread on the soil. Horse manure can be composted, and once it's well-rotted it can be used.

Green Manures

Green manures are usually plants that are grown and then dug into the soil when still green and growing, to supply the soil with organic matter, humus and other nutrients. You should select a plant that is suited to your local conditions and climate.

Examples of Green Manures

- **Alfalfa (Lucerne)**: See also Peat Alternatives page 112.
- **Rye corn.**
- **Feed oats**: Available from agricultural suppliers.
- **Annual lupins.**
- **Mustard seed**.

Make Your Own Liquid Feeds

The hard-to-eradicate weeds comfrey and nettles make a great liquid feed. Fill a large hessian sack (or old pillow case) with comfrey and nettle leaves, tie a knot in the neck of the sack, put it in a barrel of water with the lid on, and leave it to ferment for 3–4 weeks. The resulting liquor is high in potash and makes a terrific tomato and hanging-basket feed.

Compost

When waste is buried in landfill sites, methane gas (far more potent than carbon dioxide) is produced as it rots. Home composting diverts waste from landfill sites, thereby reducing the amount of methane created. A compost heap does not produce methane, so by composting as much of your waste as you can, you are not only cutting down on harmful emissions, but you also get an excellent soil conditioner, fertiliser and mulch into the bargain.

Composting Schemes

Many local authorities operate composting schemes. If your council does not operate a local composting scheme, a local community kitchen-waste collection scheme may operate instead.

Kitchen Caddy

Over 30 per cent of the average household's kitchen waste can be composted: vegetable peelings and apple cores, tea bags, shredded paper and egg cartons can all be added to the mix! Get into the habit of separating out the compostable material from the non-compostable and keep a caddy in your kitchen for it.

Bokashi Bran

Rats and mice love scraps of meat, fish and cooked foods, which is why these items should not be put in compost heaps. There is an alternative: Bokashi is a Japanese pre-composting bran inoculated with micro-organisms that pickle food waste, making it less palatable to vermin. Place food waste and leftovers into an airtight container, add a layer of the Bokashi bran and, in two weeks, you can add the pickled waste to the compost or it can be buried. Bokashi is available online at www.originalorganics.co.uk

Mix It!

Making home compost depends on getting the mix of ingredients right: green waste is quick to rot and provides important nitrogen and moisture. The browns are slower to rot but provide carbon and fibre and allow air pockets to form in the compost.

You Can Compost

The Greens

- **Fruit and vegetable scraps, salad leaves and old flowers.**
- **Coffee grounds and tea bags**: Try snipping the tea bags open to speed up the process.
- **Grass cuttings**: In small quantities.
- **Old bedding plants.**

The Browns:

- **Crushed egg, mussel or oyster shells**: These will provide valuable minerals.
- **Twigs, prunings and leaves.**
- **Shredded paper and soft cardboard**: In small amounts.
- **Human and animal hair**: Put your pet hairs to good use!
- **Vacuum dust**: But only from woollen carpets.
- **Sawdust and bark.**

Have You Thought Of?

Keeping a caddy in the kitchen? It's the ideal way to store two or three days' worth of fruit and vegetable peelings ready for composting.

You Can't Compost

- ✅ **Dog or cat excrement**: Or kitty litter.
- ✅ **Meat or fish:** Including the bones.
- ✅ **Cooked food**: But see the note on Bokashi bran on page 108.
- ✅ **Dairy.**
- ✅ **Disposable nappies.**
- ✅ **Shiny or laminated card and paper.**
- ✅ **Perennial weeds, or weeds with seed heads.**
- ✅ **Diseased plants**: They should be incinerated to stop the spread of disease.

Where to Compost

The best place for a compost bin is in a reasonably sunny site on bare soil. If you do have to put your compost bin on a hard surface, make sure there's a good layer of paper and twigs or existing compost on the bottom. Choose a site where you can add ingredients easily to the bin – and get the compost out when you need it!

How to Compost

Composting is easy! Just follow these simple steps:

1. Add waste to bin

Empty your kitchen caddy, along with your garden waste, into your compost bin. A 50-50 mix of greens and browns is the perfect recipe for a good, rich compost.

2. Aerate

Aerate your compost once in a while by turning it over using a fork or a broom handle.

3. Wait

It takes between nine and twelve months for your compost to become ready for use, so be patient.

4. Finished compost

Perfect compost is black and crumbly, with no smell, some woody brown material still visible and some worms and a few bugs that are all helping the process. Don't worry if your compost looks a little lumpy with twigs and bits of eggshell – this is perfectly normal.

5. Get gardening

Use your compost to enrich flower beds, borders and vegetable patches; mulch around plants to retain moisture; plant up patio containers or feed the lawn.

Too Green?

Slimy, wet compost surrounded by fruit flies is the result of filling a compost bin with grass cuttings, fruit and veggie peelings. There's no heat because of the lack of air! Fix this by forking the compost and adding some browns for fibre.

Too Brown?

Ideally, large amounts of leaves should be composted separately into a leaf mould. If your compost bin does have too many leaves in it, try adding some more greens, such as grass cuttings or vegetable peelings. Alternatively, you could add nettles that have been soaked in cold water – these make a great activator for a compost bin.

For Peat's Sake

If you don't make your own compost then you'll have to buy it from a garden centre, but make sure it's peat-free. Peat forms in wetland areas and is a deposit of partially decayed vegetation. Peat moss (also called sphagnum moss) can be found growing in peat bogs and is often used for lining hanging baskets and as bio-degradable pots for seedlings. Peat and peat moss have been used by gardeners to add nutrients to and assist water retention in soils. But it can take up to 3,000 years to form a wetland or peat bog, and when they're dug up for commercial use, these unique ecosystems are destroyed.

Peat Alternatives

Any compost that you buy should contain peat-free alternatives such as:

- **Coconut coir**: A waste product from coconut processing. As well as a compost and soil conditioner, it can be used as a mulch (once soaked in water, the fibres expand to up to ten times their original size) or as a liner for hanging baskets. You can also get seed pots made of coconut coir.
- **Cocoa shell**: A waste product from the manufacture of chocolate.
- **Dried alfalfa**: Like peat moss and coconut coir, alfalfa (also known as Lucerne) retains a great deal of moisture when rehydrated.
- **Mushroom compost**: One of the best fertilizers and soil conditioners available. You can dig it straight into the ground or spread it on the surface because its ingredients are almost totally decomposed.

Vermicomposting

If you don't have a garden, allotment or room for a compost heap or bin, don't despair! You can still have green fingers with a good source of compost that'll be enough for your requirements. It's easy and odour-free: it's a wormery! They're small enough to keep indoors, so even if you don't have a garden, you'll get rid of organic kitchen waste and have great-quality compost for your house plants and window boxes. There are plenty of websites packed full of information on worm composting (vermicomposting), buying or making wormeries.

Worms Worth Their Weight

Vermicomposting uses worms to break down kitchen and garden waste, and it does it faster than ordinary composting. Earthworms never sleep, so are producing compost 24/7! In the right environment, an earthworm will eat and digest up to its own body weight in a day. Earthworm castings contain more nitrogen, phosphorus and potassium than normal soil, help improve the structure of the soil, and are pH neutral. In addition to the castings, a wormery also produces a leachate – a concentrated liquid fertilizer which, when diluted for use, is suitable for both indoor and outdoor use.

What is a Wormery?

A wormery is an enclosed unit inside which are several linked compartments containing the live worms, the organic kitchen or garden waste you feed to them and processed compost in various stages of decomposition. The uppermost compartment usually has a snug biodegradable blanket on top to keep the worms nice and cosy (but not too hot, or they dehydrate and die). This layer needs to be kept moist, but can be made from fibre matting, old towels or even a thick layer of newspaper. The lid of the unit is perforated with tiny holes that let air in but stop the worms from escaping. There no smell from a wormery; if it does smell, then something is wrong.

Types of Worms

Ordinary earthworms in the garden do a fine job, but are not as efficient composters as wormery worms. The most common worm used in a wormery is the Tigerworm, also known as Brandling or Redworm (*Eisenia fetida* or *Rubellis terrestris*). Other types of worms used include *Eisenia Andrei*, which is similar to a Tigerworm but a uniform red colour; *Dendrobaena* (bigger than Tigerworms and they eat more) and *Lumbricus rubellus* (Redworms).

What They Can Eat

- ☑ **Vegetable peelings and waste.**
- ☑ **Coffee grounds.**
- ☑ **Paper.**
- ☑ **Cardboard.**
- ☑ **Eggshells.**

What They Cannot Eat

- ☑ **Meat, fish, poultry or dairy waste.**
- ☑ **Pineapple**: It contains the enzyme bromelain, which dissolves protein, so it will dissolve your worms!
- ☑ **Citrus**: And highly acidic vegetables such as onions.
- ☑ **Grass clippings**: A few are okay but too many generate heat and produce ammonia that kills the worms.

Using the Vermicompost

Because vermicompost and the leachate are very rich, the worm compost is normally mixed with other composts for use in the garden or in potting and container gardens. The recommended solution for using the leachate is one part leachate to four parts water. You can also make a liquid feed from the vermicompost by soaking the castings in water in the same proportions.

Weeds: Plants in the Wrong Places

While some weeds are invasive, others can be very beneficial and many have medicinal properties. All weeds help to break up and aerate the soil, fix nitrogen and provide food and habitats for insects, birds and other animals. When weeds die, they provide organic material for careful composting (remove seed heads to avoid more weeds). Dandelions are beloved by bees and the leaves can be used in salads; milkweed (certainly considered a weed in Australia) is the primary food source of the Monarch butterfly; clover has flowers that bees adore. It's vital that these insects are supported, as they are the main pollinators of the plants we eat. Make it your policy that if you eradicate any of these weeds, you plant some bee- and butterfly-friendly wildflowers in their place to compensate!

Organic Weed Control

The traditional tool for weeding is a hoe, but the trick is only to hoe the very top of the soil around plants: digging the hoe in more than ½ cm (¼ in) will lift weed seeds up to the surface where they will grow.

Green Alternatives

Some useful and green alternatives to chemical weed controls include:

- **Boiling water**: Pour it into the cracks/joins around paving stones on driveways and paths.
- **White vinegar**: On a sunny day, spray on undiluted white vinegar. Break the flower head off if there is one, and spray the stalk and base so it gets soaked into the roots.
- **Strong saline solution**: Good on gravel-covered areas where weeds have sprung up. Don't use this on growing areas of your garden as the salt will leach over a wider area.
- **Lemon juice**: Like vinegar, lemon juice is an acid and effective on weeds, and it breaks down very quickly.

Prevention is Better Than Cure: Mulch

In addition to the home-made weed controllers (see above), there are an increasing number of green, commercially produced preparations for weed control available. But you can reduce the amount you use by mulching around plants. This not only cuts down on weeds, but also saves water, prevents soil erosion and moderates the temperature of the soil; it also helps prevent frost heave when it's cold and slows down the warming of the soil in hot weather. Organic mulches also have the added benefit of providing nutrients to the plants you are growing.

Types of Mulch

A mulch can take many forms and be made out of a number of materials:

- **Living plant ground-cover**: Also called cover crops when referring to large-scale growing.
- **Loose particles of organic or inorganic matter spread over the soil**: Particle mulches can be made of straw or gravel, or your own, home-made compost which has cost nothing.
- **Sheets of artificial or natural materials laid on the soil surface**: These can be made of plastic, such as black polythene, woven paper, polypropylene films or geotextile fabrics (often called weed barriers or landscape fabrics).
- **Cheap alternatives**: Equally as effective are flattened cardboard cartons which can be composted afterwards. You can also use old carpet, but *not* the ones with latex backing.

Insects and Pests

While we want to encourage as many varieties of beneficial insects into our gardens as possible, we also have to be prepared to deal with the unwanted ones. Instead of chemical cocktails for killing insects and treating diseases in plants, there are many low-cost, green alternatives, including vinegar. A solution of 1 tbsp of white vinegar in 1 litre/2 pints/4 ½ cups of water makes a spray to treat rust, blackspot and powdery mildew, while mealy bugs (common on house and greenhouse plants) dabbed with a cotton wool ball soaked in white vinegar will die, along with any eggs they may have laid.

Slugs and Snails

Never use a slug or snail bait containing metaldehyde or methiocarb; they kill slugs and snails but also domestic pets, wild birds and earthworms. Iron phosphate is considered a greener alternative, but there are even safer ways to control these slimy nuisances.

Green Alternatives

- **Hunt them out**: Search for them with torches after dark. Round them up, put them in a bucket with the lid on and then take them to a duck pond: ducks love them!
- **Set traps**: Slugs and snails like to hide in dark places. Turn an empty plant pot upside down and let them hide in there, before transporting them far away.
- **Petroleum jelly**: Smear it round the sides and tops of plants pots. This does work as long as they aren't able to climb over it using a pendant leaf!

- **Copper tape**: Slugs and snails are repelled by the reaction of their bodily slime and copper. You can create a copper barrier around areas of your garden and hardware with special tape available at garden stores.

- **Brittle materials**: Crushed eggshells, gravel and pine needles are too sharp for soft under-bellies to walk over; straw and sawdust get stuck to them and stop them in their tracks.

- **Water in the morning**: Slugs and snails are most active at night and are attracted to moisture. Try watering your plants in the morning instead so the top layer of soil has a chance to dry out.

- **Frequent hoeing**: This brings their eggs to the surface where they provide a tasty treat for birds.

- **Lavender, thyme, sage, mint and geraniums**: These are all disliked by slugs and snails so you could use these as companion plants (see page 120).

- **Beer**: Sink a shallow container filled with beer into the ground. They get drunk, fall in and drown.

Ants

Ants invade for a reason, usually for food or water. The traditional method of dealing with ants is to find their nest and pour boiling through the entry hole. But unless ants are a really serious problem, you can deter them from areas of your garden instead.

Deterrants

You can create exclusion zones with:

 Vinegar.

 Lemon juice.

 Cinnamon: Sprinkle it across the threshold if ants are coming into your house.

 Bicarbonate of soda: Pour a solid line and ants won't cross it!

 Draw a chalk line: They won't cross it. This is good if they are climbing up walls.

 Coffee grounds: A ring of coffee grounds around sensitive plants also works well.

 Borax: Where ants are a serious problem, place $\frac{1}{8}$ tsp of powdered borax mixed with sugar or honey near the nest. The ants take the mix into the nest and pass it on to other ants, killing off the colony and eventually reaching the queen. Borax is relatively harmless to larger animals, but in sufficient doses it can kill, so be careful about storage, use and placement, and keep it out of reach of small children.

Companion Planting

This is is where you inter-plant one species of plant (say, a vegetable) with another. There are many examples of companion planting combinations on green gardening websites, so have a look. A surprising number are familiar bedding plants that will add an extra splash of colour in the vegetable garden! Marigolds deter slugs and are said to be good at keeping down carrot fly.

Living Roofs

Cities and towns place a great pressure on the environment. In a bid to counteract this impact, many people are installing a green or living roof. Vegetated roofs have been in use for a long time, from the Hanging Gardens of Babylon to the turfed roof houses of Ireland and Scandinavia. Some cities, like Portland, Oregon, USA, are leading the way in greening roofs.

Why Not?

They don't require a huge space – you can make a green roof on a garden shed and, contrary to belief, the roof doesn't need to be flat. If you've got a flat-roofed extension that needs repairing or replacing, then why not make it a living one?

The Advantages of Living Roofs

There are several advantages over ordinary roofs:

- **Extended roof life**: Green roofs protect the waterproofing membrane from UV light degradation and damaged caused by extremes of temperatures (heat and frost damage). Green roofs are great at keeping a flat roof watertight for much longer: up to 60 years.
- **Insulation:** They cut down on heat loss in winter and act as a coolant in the summer, which means energy savings.
- **Encourages biodiversity**: And create safe havens for pollinating insects.
- **Sound-proofing**: The mix of soil, plants and trapped air in green roofs makes effective sound-proofing.
- **Albedo effect**: Green roofs can help reduce the albedo effect, created when hard

surfaces in towns and cities absorb solar radiation and reflect it back into the atmosphere, creating heat islands.

✅ **Store rainwater**: This then evaporates back into the atmosphere, which means that storm and rainwater run-off from roofs is slower, reducing the likelihood of local flooding.

✅ **Improves air quality**: They reduce CO_2 in the atmosphere and produce oxygen instead.

Green Roof Installation

There are a number of companies specializing in the installation of living roofs; check them out on the Internet. But there are also numerous sites to help the competent DIYer, too. You could make a start with the garden shed!

What You Need

The main components of a living roof are:

✅ **A timber frame**: This holds the roof elements in place.

✅ **Root membrane**: You can use pond liner or a 300 micron damp-proof membrane.

✅ **Filter sheet**: This stops the fine material leaving the roof, holding in the fine soil or growing medium and letting water pass through.

✅ **Moisture blanket**: A woolly fleece that holds water. You can buy geotextile membranes, but for a shed roof, old towels, blankets or cardboard will do.

✅ **Substrate**: What the plants will grow in – a mix of recycled, crushed concrete or brick, limestone chippings, gravel, clay pellets or lightweight perlite. On top of this you will need a layer of sand, soil or a mix of both.

✅ **Plants**: The type of plants you grow on your living roof will depend on the type of substrate and the substrate depth. Read on for more details.

What to Plant on the Living Roof

Sedums are amongst the most popular plants for living roofs as they are low-maintenance and need minimal weeding. Sedums are hardy, evergreen succulents (they store water in their leaves) and many species will flower in summer, attracting butterflies, ladybirds and other insects. In addition, you can add wildflower seeds, which will provide nectar for bees, butterflies and other insects, as well as seeds in winter for birds. Cowslip (*Primula veris*), harebells (*Campanula rotundifolia*), thyme (*thymus*) and small scabious (*Scabioisa columbaria*) are ideal; you could also grow thrift (*Armeria*) and saxifrages.

Checklist

- **Grow flowers**: Even if these are in a window box, hanging basket or container garden.
- **Grow food**: Choose from cabbages, carrots, peas, beans, lettuces, potatoes or fruit.
- **Choose organic fertilizers**: Synthetic fertilizers are cocktails of chemicals.
- **Get composting**: This will reduce your household waste and return nutrients to your garden.
- **Start a wormery**: Dispose of food waste even if you do not have a garden.
- **Practice organic weed control**: Use a green alternative to chemical weed controls or mulch around plants to prevent weed growth in the first place.
- **Deal with unwanted insects by companion planting**: Look on the Internet to find out which plants deter which insects.
- **Consider a living roof**: Create a haven for insects and improve the air quality in your town.

Food & Drink

Organic Food and Drink

It's a fact: we have to eat to live. Over the past couple of decades consumers have become increasingly aware of the 'value' of our food. Many consumers have become aware of a food's nutritional value, or lack of it, in order to improve their own health and wellbeing, but increasingly consumers are also becoming more aware of the impact their consumption has on the environment, the origins of their food and drink, the welfare and rights of the farmers and growers, and the welfare of animals. There is now a wide range of certified and clearly labelled foodstuffs available in the market that allow for socially conscious consuming.

What is Organic?

The term 'organic' refers to the way agricultural products are grown, processed, distributed, labelled and sold, so consumers are assured that the product maintains the organic integrity that began at source, on the farm. Organic production is based on a system of farming that maintains and replenishes the soil without the use of toxic or persistent pesticides and fertilizers (those that remain in the soil long after their initial application).

Other Organic Standards

Organic foods should also be minimally processed, without artificial ingredients or preservatives. Organic foods must also be produced without the use of:

- Antibiotics.
- Synthetic hormones.
- Genetic engineering.
- Sewage sludge.
- Irradiation.
- Cloned animals (or using their products).

Organic Certification

In the early days of the organic food revolution most organic farmers would have sold their produce directly at the door in farm shops or at farmers' markets, so organic certification was not deemed necessary; it was a matter of trust based on a direct relationship between the producer and the consumer. But as more and more consumers began to seek out organic foods, the supermarkets saw an opportunity to increase sales in this sector. Consequently, a third-party regulatory certification scheme was needed so that consumers could be protected from bogus organic claims. Organic farming and food production have to meet stringent standards and, to ensure the practice is organic, systems of certification have been established. However, requirements do vary from country to country, so you really need to read the labels carefully.

Why Go Organic?

Despite some of the confusions about degrees of organic-ness, the benefits – to humans, to nature and to animals – are considerable. Many claim that organic produce has superior flavour but this is subjective, and even the best produce in the world can be ruined by the worst cook! The jury is also out on claims for organic food being more nutritious. However, if you take into account some of the benefits listed overleaf, organic food will probably do you less harm than industrially produced food.

Naturally Beneficial

The benefits of organic food and drinks are:

- **GM-free**: Organic foods (for both human and animal consumption) are GM-free.
- **Contains far fewer artificial additives**: If any.
- **BSE-free**: Organic meat is BSE (Bovine Spongiform Encephalopathy or 'mad cow disease') free. BSE can cause the related disease CJD (Creutzfeld Jacob Disease) in humans and is caused by livestock feed containing animal proteins.
- **Free from synthetic hormones and growth promoters**: Antibiotics are used sparingly as a specific treatment and not as a preventative measure as in factory-farmed livestock.
- **Farming methods create less impact on the environment**: This is at both micro and macro levels. No pesticides, herbicides or artificial fertilizers means there are no damaging toxins released into the air, water, soil or food chain and nor are humans exposed to them in the course of their work.
- **Higher animal welfare standards**: Certified organic livestock enjoy a much higher standard of treatment.

Healthy Life, Healthy Planet

Every time a consumer makes the conscious decision to buy organic food and drink, it is one step further forward towards a healthier life and a healthier planet.

Ethical and Fairly Traded Food

Ethical consumerism is buying products (and services) that are made or provided with minimal harm to, or exploitation of, humans, animals and/or the environment. Ethical consumerism can also be practised through moral boycotts, such as refusing to buy goods or services from particular companies whose practices are perceived as unfair, or by positive buying (favouring and purchasing ethical products, be they Fairtrade, cruelty-free, organic, recycled, reused or locally produced).

Ethical Trading

The Ethical Trading Initiative (ETI), which was set up in 1998, is an alliance of companies, NGOs (Non-Governmental Organisations) and international trades unions working to promote ethical consumerism and ensure decent working conditions for the people who produce the goods we buy.

Consuming Ethically

As ethical consumers, we need to look for the following labels, which will indicate that some reliable validation has taken place:

- **Fairtrade (Fair Trade Certified in the US).**
- **Social Accountability 8000**: An international standard for improving working conditions based on the principles of the 13 International Human Rights Conventions.
- **Certified Organic.**
- **Free Range.**
- **Vegan and vegetarian suitable.**
- **Halaal**: A religious standard.
- **Kosher**: A religious standard.
- **Line-caught fish.**
- **Dolphin-friendly.**
- **Rainforest Alliance Certified.**
- **Recycled.**

Fairtrade

Fairtrade food has gone from marginal to mainstream. In 2003 there were just 150 Fairtrade products; now there are more than 1,000 products, ranging from food to footballs. Fairtrade seeks to empower producers in developing countries and promote sustainability by paying fair prices for an increasingly wide variety of products notably: bananas, coffee, cocoa, sugar, tea, honey, nuts, spices, rice and fresh fruits as well as flowers, cotton and handicrafts.

Beneficial to All

Fairtrade foods are sold at a minimum rate so the producers (both the farmers and the hired labour) are able to make enough to live on and continue production, thereby improving living and working conditions in the future. The prices paid and the trading terms (which include prepayment where required) are determined not by current *market* conditions but by factoring in economic, social and environmental well-being; Fairtrade guarantees farmers a long-term fixed price for their crops regardless of ups and downs in the world market. The Fairtrade scheme also pays a 'social premium' that is invested in community projects such as healthcare, schools and adult literacy programmes.

Fairtrade and the Environment

As well as promoting an ethical trade, Fairtrade foods also come with environmental benefits as there are some restrictions on the use of synthetic chemical fertilizers and pesticides; these have encouraged some Fairtrade producers to become wholly organic producers. Fairtrade proponents include well-known brands as well as a wide range of international organisations, such as Oxfam and Amnesty International. The Fairtrade Labelling Organisation is the largest and most widely recognised standard setting and certification body for fair-trade goods, regularly inspecting and certifying producers in more than 50 countries.

Have You Thought Of?

Looking at the labels of the food you buy and considering where it comes from and how it has been produced?

Local and Seasonal Food

Supermarkets, with their huge range of air-freighted fruit and vegetables, mean that we have lost touch with the seasons. We can buy what we want when we want, such as strawberries or fresh peas in the middle of winter. Such produce has an impact on our environment – think of the fertilizers and pesticides used in growing, the emissions caused during transport and the amount and type of packaging needed to protect the produce during transit and in warehousing, not to mention the waste involved. Add to these concerns about the working and pay conditions of the labour (and the animal welfare) in the countries of origin, and it's not surprising that many consumers are looking very carefully at what goes in their shopping baskets.

Think Global, Act Local and Seasonal

The Internet has been a valuable tool for producers and consumers in going green, not only in providing communication and information to a global marketplace, but also in helping to identify local initiatives, producers and suppliers. Using the Internet, consumers can find food suppliers on their doorstep. In the USA, using the NRDC (National Resources Defense Council) website, you can type in your home state and the season, and find out what's available and where to purchase it. In Canada, www.eatwellguide.org site helps consumers find organic, sustainable, local, seasonal produce in their home province. In Australia, a good site for local and seasonal food and drink is www.naturalstrategies.com.au. In the UK and Ireland, www.localfoodadvisor.com is a useful site. Each has links to other useful sites, including tips on cooking and menu suggestions, nutrition and health, as well as the greater benefits of local and seasonal produce for producers and consumers.

Farm Stores, Farmers' Markets and Co-operatives

Instead of driving to a supermarket, have a day out in the countryside: you don't even have to go deep into the wilds to find fruit, eggs, honey, flowers and plants, as many small producers often have excess produce for sale outside their front doors. For meat and dairy produce produced locally and organically, farm stores offer a wide range of produce. And if you can't get to the countryside, let it come to you: farmers' markets now take place in cities and towns on a weekly or monthly basis and farmers' co-operative stores are also gaining a foothold on the high street.

Vegetable Box Schemes

The central principle of the veg box scheme is to deliver a box of fresh, locally produced, seasonal organic produce to the consumer. Because the contents of the boxes are seasonal, you generally get what you are given, although many schemes now let you omit some vegetables and stock up with others. Box schemes are beneficial to local growers and producers, and to the consumer and the environment:

- **Growers can respond directly to customer requests**: There is less waste as the growers know their harvest will be sold, rather than having to let it rot because a supermarket has changed its order.
- **All the produce is sold**: There's no grading out for size or shape so it fits supermarket packaging!
- **There's little or no packaging waste**: Even the box is returnable and refillable.
- **The middleman is cut out**: So there's greater profit for the grower and cheaper prices for the consumer.
- **Consumers have a supply of local and seasonal produce**: From a known grower with whom they can have direct contact.

Pick Your Own

In addition to farm stores, many producers also operate 'pick your own' sites, especially for fruits and berries. In North America, these are known as 'U-pick fields'. In Britain there are more than 1,000 pick-your-own sites, with an increasing number offering certified organic produce. Some sites have shops, butchers, bakeries, restaurants, craft and garden centres, while others are more like working farms – with some even offering camping, known as 'pitch and pick'. Pick-your-own is one method of eating good-quality, locally produced and seasonal produce and you only buy what you need, so you cut down on waste.

Tips for Picking Your Own

- **Pick your own at organic farms and sites**: Get pesticide- and fertilizer-free produce.
- **Go to the furthest points in the fields**: Families with young children may not be able to go very far and lazy-bones just want to pick and go, so the areas nearest the entrance (usually nearest the car park!) will be pretty bereft of produce.
- **Pick the seasonal best**: Look for the farmer's or grower's signs telling you which types of fruits or vegetables are at their seasonal best; different cultivars ripen at different times and, consequently, they develop their flavours at different times too.
- **Wear stout shoes or Wellington boots**: In Britain at least, you can probably guarantee that it will have rained at some time before you arrive to pick your own so the ground will be wet and muddy, especially near the entrance!

Slow Food

The Slow Food Movement was founded in 1986 in Bra, near Turin, Italy, initially to combat 'fast food' and to preserve the local cultures of cuisine, along with the food, plants and seeds, animals and farming within eco-regions. The movement has since grown to include nearly 100,000 members in over 120 countries. It is organized into *convivia* (local chapters); you can find one near you by going to www.slowfood.com.

Go Slow!

The movement's objectives include:

- **Developing 'Arks of Tastes'**: For each eco-region, where local foods and cooking styles are celebrated.
- **Preserving and promoting local and traditional foods.**
- **Organizing processing for small–scale producers.**
- **Organizing celebrations of local cuisines**: Such as the Feast of Fields held in some Canadian cities.
- **Educating consumers**: About the drawbacks of commercial factory-farming.
- **Lobbying**: Against the use of pesticides and genetic engineering.
- **Preserving heritage and heirloom varieties**: By forming and maintaining seed banks and promoting bio-diversity in the food supply.
- **Encouraging ethical buying in local markets.**
- **Encouraging sustainably produced food and drink**: Which does not harm the environment, human health or animal welfare.

Food Miles

A food mile or kilometre is the distance food travels from the farmer who produces it
to the consumer who eats it. Sounds simple, but the journey often includes the miles from
the producer to the processor, the processor to the retailer, and from the store to our kitchen
cupboard. Food miles aren't just relevant for fresh produce like fruit, vegetables and meat, but
also many processed foods such as ready-meals, vegetable oils, flour and sugar.

Cutting the Miles

Have a look at an atlas of the world while inspecting your cupboards, then add up the miles all
the food has travelled! The most practical way to reduce food miles is to shop locally, but you
could also reduce the number of miles between the store and your home by shopping online
and having the produced delivered; one van or truck serving a whole neighbourhood is better
than several cars all travelling to the supermarket. Who knows, we may see the return of the
more personalized service from our stores, including the boy (or girl) on the delivery bicycle!

What You Can Do

There are a number of ways in which the green consumer can reduce the number of miles their food has travelled:

 Actively buy food that is in season.

 Look closely at the country-of-origin labels: And make your purchases accordingly.

 Shop at farmers' markets, farm shops and pick-your-own farms.

 Cut down on the number of trips you make to the supermarket: Make use of a box scheme to provide local, organic foods on a regular basis instead.

 Grow your own fruit and vegetables: See the chapter on Gardens page 94 and, if you have the space, why not keep a few hens too!

 Choose fairly traded: For products that cannot be produced locally, such as coffee.

Food for Free!

Some of the finest seasonal and locally produced food is free. Did you know that there are over 15,000 edible plants, yet we only consume around 25 of them: the average range that stores and supermarkets provide us with. Rural cooks have used the countryside as an extra larder for a long time but today, with the interest in environmental issues as well as a desire for more interesting foods, foraging is becoming increasingly popular. Wild, edible food plants make a great addition to a healthy lifestyle and they are local and sustainable, which means you are minimizing your food miles and your carbon footprint.

More Than Just Blackberries

We're all familiar with blackberries growing freely and they are probably number one on the free food list, but did you know that nettles are edible? There are also wild mushrooms, garlic, wood sorrel, samphire, elderflowers (and elderberries), sloes (blackthorn berries) and even dandelion leaves out there waiting to be enjoyed.

Foraging

The rules of foraging are simple:

- **Be aware**: Novice foragers are advised to find a knowledgeable fellow enthusiast to accompany them on forages. Always carry a plant guide to help with identification, and be aware that not all the parts of some plants are edible. Organized fungi forages are the best way to become knowledgeable about which mushrooms can be eaten safely.
- **If you don't know it's safe to eat, leave it alone**: Even if you come home empty-handed, you'll have enjoyed a great day out!
- **Avoid hedgerows near heavy traffic**: Or that may have been sprayed with pesticides.
- **Stay within the law**: Show respect for the land and never uproot wild plants without the permission of landowners.
- **Avoid disturbing the habitat of animals or birds**: And in certain countries, make sure you are aware of wild animals (boars, bears, etc) living in the vicinity.
- **Only pick what you need**: This means less food is wasted, but it also means you won't prevent the plant from reproducing, or stop animals from feeding.

Freeganism

In the 1990s, groups such as Food Not Bombs served free vegan and vegetarian food that was rescued from supermarkets, and freeganism was born. This anti-consumerist lifestyle involves salvaging discarded but unspoiled food from supermarkets (known as 'dumpster diving'); the food may have passed its sell-by date, but it hasn't passed its eat-by date. The practice has now extended to 'guerrilla gardening', where vacant plots of land, including roundabouts, verges and overgrown abandoned gardens, are reclaimed and planted with fruit and vegetables for community distribution, often through Really Free Markets or Free Stores where people can exchange food, goods and services (such as bike repair and rebuilds from spare parts) outside a money-based economy.

Meat and Poultry

Free range is a method of animal husbandry where the animals are allowed to roam freely instead of being penned or contained in any way; it may apply to meat, eggs or dairy farming. Free range used to be the norm, until the development of barbed and chicken wire. Once again though, the interpretation of free range varies from country to country: in the USA, for example, there is no specific definition for free-range beef, lamb, pork or other non-poultry product, and there is no minimum size to the range or the amount of space given to each animal in order for them to be called free range. Consequently, claims and labelling using the term 'free range' are, as yet, unregulated; the US certification body, the USDA, relies on producer testimonials to support claims. In countries where ranching or herding is practised, free-range livestock are allowed to roam without being fenced in, while in other places, the pastures may be fenced in.

Meat

Some of the most serious environmental problems we are experiencing today can be linked to the growing consumption of meat. As the appetite for meat-based protein grows in both the west and in developing countries, so the need for more land and other resources increases. Consequently, we now see huge areas of deforestation (not just for cattle grazing, but also for the growing of livestock feed) which impacts negatively in terms of water pollution (from chemicals and from animal faeces), air pollution and local biodiversity, which in turn aggravate global warming. While many have eschewed meat and animal products completely, ethical omnivores are taking steps to reduce the amount of such produce they consume, and opt for organic, free-range and, increasingly, humanely raised meat.

Humanely Raised Meat

Consumers who are already buying locally produced, seasonal, free-range and organic food are also willing to pay a little more for their meat in the knowledge that the animal didn't suffer on its way to becoming their dinner. There are some good reasons, ranging from ethics to environmentalism, for buying humanely raised over traditional or factory-farmed animal products. Typically, animals humanely raised are provided with more space; on some farms (though not all), the animals rotate through fields with other species and plants, in the hope that

this will create a better farm environment and a healthier animal. Instead of being given growth hormones, animals are allowed to mature at their own rate and are handled gently through their lives and the slaughter process.

Local and Trusted

Another benefit of humanely raised meat is that the (often small-scale) farmers are willing to meet with consumers who want to see for themselves the conditions in which their animals are raised. This is probably the most reliable way to source your food ethically, but third-party verification from a reputable organization is becoming easier to find. In the UK he RSPCA has a labelling scheme called Freedom Foods and the US has the Animal Welfare Approved certification scheme. Locally produced, humanely reared and slaughtered animals may cost the consumer more, but the benefits to the animal, the farmer and the environment are well worth the additional expense if you must eat meat and animal products.

Poultry

Until the discovery of Vitamins A and D in the 1920s, free-range poultry was the norm as the hens needed green feed and sunshine to provide them with their vitamins. Once the vitamins could be synthesized, chickens got cooped up and packed into high-density floor confinement or cages. Again, what makes for a free range-chicken – or indeed a free-range egg – varies across the world. In the US the fuzziness of the term 'free range' allows for poultry and eggs to be labelled as 'cage-free', 'free-running', 'naturally nested' and 'free-roaming'. These terms are in fact simply alternatives to the technical term 'high-density floor confinement', which is the complete antithesis of free range!

Eggheads: Read the Numbers

Under European Union regulations, egg farming is classified into four categories: organic, free range, barn and caged, each category being more progressively strict in terms of the

hen's wellbeing and subsequent egg quality. Mandatory labelling on eggshells attributes a number – the first digit on the stamp refers to the category: 0 for organic; 1 for free range; 2 for barn and 3 for cages. Understanding this means you can open a box of eggs and quickly see that they are in the correctly labelled boxes.

Free-range Eggs vs Organic Eggs

Free-range eggs labelled as such are are not necessarily organic. To be an organic egg:

- **Hens are only fed organic feed**: They are not fed any animal by-products or GM crops, which *is* permitted with free-range hens.
- **No antibiotics are allowed except in emergencies**: Again, antibiotics are administered in free-range hens, often to the same levels as in factory-farmed hens.
- **Organic hens must live cage–free**: But it is important to note that they are still raised in confinement although they are free-roaming through barns.
- **Organic hens must have access to the outdoors**: Doors are opened periodically to allow the hens into a fenced enclosure.
- **Organic egg producers may not *induce* a moult**: Which occurs naturally when a hen is laying well. This is permitted in free-range egg farming.
- **Beak cutting and wing trimming are prohibited**: This practice is permitted in free-range egg farming.

Your Own Hens

In truth, the best eggs always come from your own hens but, when you need to buy eggs, whenever possible choose organic free-range eggs for the very best of both worlds!

Fish

Over-fishing and pollution have seriously impacted on the size of fish stocks and the health of marine life. Fish – and their omega-3 oils – are good for us, but not when they come with a side order of mercury or other environmental toxins and habitat destruction! For consumers, the green alternatives include organically farmed fish, line-caught fish (which targets particular species and avoids catching others as would happen in trawling) and sustainable fishing.

Farmed Fish

Organic fish is farmed fish and includes trout and salmon along with mussels and other shellfish. Just as in other organic farms, pesticides, dyes and antibiotics are not permitted. There is debate, however, as to whether farmed fish can really be organic as the organic principles demand that livestock should be able to follow its natural behaviour patterns and be kept as close to natural stocking densities as possible. This works fine for some fish, like mussels, trout and other freshwater fish, but the natural density for salmon is near impossible to achieve, so perhaps a truly organically farmed salmon is doubtful.

Sustainable Fishing

In addition to maintaining (and increasing) fish stocks, sustainable fishing involves ensuring that fishing does not negatively impact on other marine life and habitats. There are now many organisations worldwide that aim to promote sustainable fishing, such as the Marine Stewardship Council (MSC). The MSC currently certifies 35 fisheries from around the world, providing around 1,900 certified fish products – including fresh, frozen, smoked, canned and fish oil dietary supplements – that carry the MSC logo on their packaging. If you want seafood from a sustainable source that doesn't over-fish and exhaust stock, or affect the marine habitat, look for the MSC logo on the products. You'll find yourself spoiled for choice as the catch includes Alaskan pollock, salmon from the USA, rock lobster from Western Australia and hoki from New Zealand, as well as mackerel, herrings and langoustines from the UK.

Food Waste

The best thing that can happen to our food is that it is eaten and enjoyed so there's no waste, apart from the obvious inedible bits like banana skins and eggshells (although even these can be recycled on the compost heap). Reducing food waste really starts before the shopping trip: the weekly shopping trip often results in a trolley full of food that would, in fact, last a month. Before you shop, why not sit down and plan in advance the week's meals, including packed lunches. This will allow you to think about quantities, portion sizes and seasonal produce, and help stick to a budget, too.

Shop Wisely

When you do go shopping, take your list with you and stick to it! Never go food shopping when you're hungry: you'll fill you basket with eat-me-now produce and stray from the green path!

Tips to Avoid Food Waste

- **Avoid BOGOF (Buy One Get One Free) offers**: Unless they can be stored long-term or frozen.
- **Check the dates**: Buy food with the longest shelf life so if you change your plans, you can still use it later on. (See the next page for more on sell-by dates.)
- **Use local butchers, fishmongers and greengrocers**: Not only does this cut down your food miles, but here you can often buy individual items or the exact number or weight you require. If you live alone, it makes sense to buy one carrot rather than a big bag, or two sausages instead of a packet of eight (although you can eat them cold and take them in your lunch box!)

Weigh out ingredients: When you cook from scratch, weigh the ingredients to reduce leftovers, or to increase the volumes to make extra to freeze or use as the next day's lunch.

Get your freezer organized: Make sure produce is labelled clearly with dates and put a contents label on the door or lid telling you what's in there and when you need to use it by. That way you won't buy more of the same thing and you won't have to open the freezer door, letting the cold air out!

Feed your pets: If you don't eat the leftovers, don't forget that your dog or cat might enjoy them! Dogs are pretty omnivorous but they should never be given chocolate as it is poisonous to them. Cats are either fuss-pots and picky eaters or sneaky thieves, so be prepared for them either to turn their noses up or have stolen the leftovers from under your nose!

Grow your own: You'll understand the time it takes to produce our food, but because the flavour is more intense, you'll probably eat less of it!

Best Before, Display Until/Sell-by and Use-by Dates

Much of the food that is wasted is thrown out because we look at the label, see some dates, glance at the calendar and presume that the food is off or has gone bad. As consumers, we need to get label-savvy and understand the meanings of each term. This will ensure that when we shop, we get the freshest possible produce, and when we store food, we know exactly when it can be safely eaten.

Best Before

Best before dates are usually found on goods with a longer shelf life, such as frozen, canned or dried goods, and refer to *quality* rather than safety. If the product hasn't been thawed out and refrozen, the can isn't bulging or rusty, and the packaging is intact on dried goods, then it should be safe to eat, although the contents may have lost some of their flavour, texture or colour. The *exception* to this rule is eggs: never eat eggs after their best before date.

Display Until and Sell By

Display-until and sell-by dates often appear near or next to the best-before or use-by date. These are there to help with stock control, so they are instructions to the store, not the shopper! It is these products that are often reduced in price at the end of the day.

Use By

Use-by dates are key to food safety; they are most usually found on raw and cooked meats, soft cheeses and dairy-based produce. Never eat produce after this date but do look carefully at the storage instructions when you buy such produce, because it may be possible for it to be frozen to extend its life for use at a later date.

Leftovers

An incredible amount of edible food is wasted, usually because people don't have the time or inclination to get to grips with leftovers. Going green in the kitchen by reducing the amount of food waste not only saves money and reduces the amount of food ending up in landfills, it also makes for much more variety at mealtimes.

Lovely Leftovers

Try some of these clever ideas to use up what may otherwise end up in the bin:

 Compost: Inedible parts of produce, such as apple cores, vegetable peelings, banana skins and other organic waste, should be recycled and added to the compost heap.

 **Soup**: Bones and skin (from chicken, fish and meat) can be turned into soups and stocks, along with some of those vegetable scraps.

Ripe fruits: These can be baked in pies, stewed into compotes, made into jam or mixed with yoghurt into a healthy smoothie (free from preservatives, artificial colours, stabilisers and the wasted plastic bottle too!)

Vegetables: These can be pickled or made into chutney and savoury preserves.

Dry bread: The last pieces of dry bread can be toasted, made into bread pudding, turned into breadcrumbs or croutons.

Wine: The last bits of wine in the bottom of glasses or bottles can be frozen into wine cubes for adding oomph to stews.

Store It

Millions of tons of food is wasted every day, with most of it ending up in landfill sites. Buried underground in airless conditions, as it rots, organic waste produces methane gas, one of the most problematic of the greenhouse gasses. Sensible composting of household waste can help, but the most sensible thing to do is to cut down on what we waste in the first place. Sensible storing and preserving fresh produce (by chilling, freezing, bottling, canning and pickling) means that we have a ready supply of nutritious food.

The Store Cupboard

A store cupboard should be dry, cool and closed. To keep your stock healthy, write the sell-by or use-by dates clearly on packets and tins and rotate your stock so the oldest purchases are used first; that way they don't exceed their dates and there's no waste!

Cans, Bottles and Jars

Here are some other top tips for storage:

- **Treat as fresh**: Once they're opened, bottled and canned foodstuffs should be treated as if they were fresh foods.
- **Store in the fridge**: If you don't use all the contents of a can, transfer the balance into a different container and store in the fridge.
- **Don't store herbs and pulses in glass jars**: The light permeates and destroys the colour and flavour of herbs and makes pulses' skins tough!

Storing Fresh Fruit and Vegetables

Too often, perfectly edible fruit and vegetables are wasted because they've become over-ripe or perhaps have a blemish. This is where canny cooks start making soups and smoothies! And don't forget that if you have bought organic vegetables, you can freeze the peelings for use in soups at a later date.

Tips for Storing Fruit and Vegetables

- **Ripen avocadoes**: Avocados only ripen when they've been picked, and the ripening processed is slowed down because they are shipped in refrigerated conditions. You can keep avocados unripe by keeping them cool, or speed up the ripening by keeping them in a warm place, putting them in a plastic bag with a piece of banana peel, or just burying them at the bottom of a fruit bowl!

- **Store apples on a tray or rack**: So they don't touch each other. This prevents any 'bruises' from contaminating the others.

- **Don't store melons in the fridge**: They'll transfer their scent to everything!

- **Banana skins tell you how ripe they are**: Green tints mean they're not quite ripe but will be ready after a day or two in a warm place. Brown spots tell you it's ready for eating; the more spots, the riper and softer the banana. You can store bananas in the fridge to stop them ripening, but their skins will darken.

- **Storing potatoes**: Stop potatoes sprouting by storing them in a cool, dry place with a few apples.

- **Buy loose olives**: Then label and date a jar, transfer the olives and pour in enough olive oil to cover them. You can keep topping up the jar for about nine months.

- **Don't wash celery until you need it**: It loses its flavour.

Cut off the leafy green tops from carrots: This growing end continues to draw water and nutrients from the root – the bit you want to eat! Like all root veg, carrots keep best in cool, dry and dark places with good ventilation.

Lemons: After you've cut a lemon in half, place it cut side down on a plate and cover with a glass. Store whole lemons in the egg shelves of the fridge.

Eggs: Store eggs pointed end down in a bowl at the bottom of the fridge and they'll last for three weeks.

Garlic cloves and bulbs: These are best kept in a cool dry place, but you can save time and energy if you peel the cloves and pop them in a jar of olive oil. This will extend the garlic's life and give you a supply of garlic-flavoured oil too!

Meat, fish and poultry: Surface moisture on meat, fish and poultry is a breeding ground for bacteria. Remove it from the packaging, pat the flesh dry with paper and place each piece into a separate closed container with the lid slightly off, or on a plate covered loosely with a bowl to allow the air to circulate freely.

Never re-freeze defrosted food: Food can be defrosted, cooked and then frozen, but twice is the maximum number of times food can be cooked or heated.

Food Packaging Waste

The global food packaging industry is worth billions, but did you realise that up to 50 per cent of the price of food we buy can be down to its packaging! The more we buy, the more we eat, and the more packaging we throw away – and so the financial and environmental costs to our world keep on increasing. Nevertheless, there are some good reasons why food is packaged: for hygiene control and to prevent contamination; to prolong the life of food; for safe transportation; and to give consumers information about the contents.

Cutting Down on Waste Food Packaging

The first step is to get rid of our reliance on plastic shopping bags. The town of Modbury in Devon, UK, was the first place to set an example by becoming a plastic-bag-free zone. San Francisco and Paris have followed, and Australia and China are now discussing total bans. Many farmers' markets across the globe have stopped giving free bags to customers.

Unwrapped

There are also other ways in which we as consumers can cut down on the amount of food packaging waste:

- **Think before you buy**: Do you need it? If not, leave it on the shelf; you'll save money and have less waste.
- **Choose larger sizes**: Rather than individually packed portions. Try buying a big pot of yoghurt and decanting it into portion-sized reusable jars at home.
- **Take your bags to the shops with you**: And use them!

Carry a spare bag with you at all times: For those impulse purchases!

Buy fruit and vegetables loose or in paper bags: The bags are useful to take packed lunches in. Or join a box scheme where fresh, seasonal organic fruit and vegetables are delivered to your home (or office) in a reusable carton or box.

Look for biodegradable packaging: Choose cardboard or cornstarch-based containers instead of plastics or polystyrene.

Find a milkman to deliver to your doorstep: It's the best way to recycle those milk bottles,

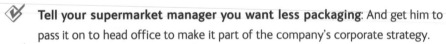

Have You Thought Of?

Avoiding takeaways? Not only are they unhealthy, all that polystyrene and foam is bad for the environment too.

Tell your supermarket manager you want less packaging: And get him to pass it on to head office to make it part of the company's corporate strategy.

Get a lunch box and a vacuum flask or insulated travel mug: Even if you buy a takeaway sandwich and a coffee from a store, ask them not to wrap it but put it straight into your box or cup. Most places will be happy to do it – it's less work for them, it saves time and it saves them money!

Recycle: Make sure any food packaging that does come home goes into the recycling.

Use your imagination: Polystyrene and plastic trays for meat and fish can be rinsed out and used for planting seeds; cardboard egg cartons are great little seedling pots; compost paper and cardboard; or make papier-maché to fill the gaps between your floors and walls to keep out drafts!

Grow your own fruit and vegetables: Or pick your own or go foraging, but remember to take a reusable bag with you!

Checklist

- ☑ **Consider switching to organic, Fairtrade and ethically produced food:** There are many benefits for you and the environment.
- ☑ **Buy local, seasonal food:** It will be cheaper and won't have travelled across the world to your plate.
- ☑ **Can you afford free-range meat and poultry?:** It may be worth a little extra money to know that your dinner was raised humanely.
- ☑ **Avoid food waste:** Plan ahead, thinking about meals and portions, and your shopping bill may also be reduced.
- ☑ **Store your food correctly:** This will prolong its life and reduce food waste.
- ☑ **Try and cut down on food packaging waste:** How can you reduce, reuse and recycle your food packaging waste?

Fashion & Beauty

Green Fashion

Consumers want to be fashionable. However, as they learn more about the origins of the items they buy, they also want their clothes to be ethically traded and environmentally friendly. Increasingly, fashion designers, beauty companies and manufacturers are responding to ethical consumers and their needs; it's now possible to get green stylish clothing ranging from simple T-shirts to high-fashion outfits.

The Fashion Cycle

The modern fashion cycle of seasonal change (autumn/winter and spring/summer collections) was invented by Christian Dior in Paris as a marketing strategy to increase sales of French fashion after the Second World War. The cycle subsequently filtered down to the ready-to-wear and high-street producers, encouraging us to become conspicuous consumers. Perfectly wearable clothes, shoes and accessories are discarded because they are no longer in fashion.

Fashion Initiatives

Fortunately, interest in fashion and design has encouraged a range of initiatives including dress swaps and second-hand designer boutiques. The interest in vintage looks and classic garments has gone some way towards helping the recycling of clothes; such garments are now sought after by consumers, designers and even celebrities. Even charity stores now boast designer rails with premium price tags! Old is the new New!

Have You Thought Of?

Using your clothes as cleaning cloths when they get beyond repair?

Ethical Fashion

The fashion industry is, unfortunately, one of the most exploitative – of both people and the environment. With a great deal of the manufacturing of garments outsourced to Asia, North Africa and parts of South America, far away from the fashion markets where the garments are sold, inhuman working conditions, poverty wages, child labour and environmental damage are widespread.

Different Sources

One of the problems with the fashion industry is that the different parts of a garment may come from a variety of different countries, which makes it difficult to monitor the environmental and social conditions at every stage of production. This means that at the moment there isn't a certified ethical guarantee for fashion goods. Until that happens, consumers need to make their own evaluations about the garments and the companies they buy them from.

Check Them Out

Checking out company websites for their buying procedures or mission statements is a good starting point; these should state their green credentials or efforts. Fashion customers can look out for Fairtrade, organic or eco-labels and certification or, alternatively, affiliation with ethical and fair-trade bodies, such as the Ethical Fashion Forum (EFF) or the International Fair Trade Association (IFAT).

Green Garments

Across the world, designers and manufacturers are becoming committed to developing sweatshop-free, organic, ethical, sustainable and fashionable clothes. In the UK, the Ethical Fashion Forum (EFF) lists a growing number of designers and fashion labels committed to ethical and sustainable fashion. In the USA, TransFair, the fair-trade certifier that initially focussed on food certification, has extended its interest into certification for garment factories, and there are several sizeable apparel companies dedicated to fair-trade. For shoppers this means fashionable clothing that doesn't cost the earth.

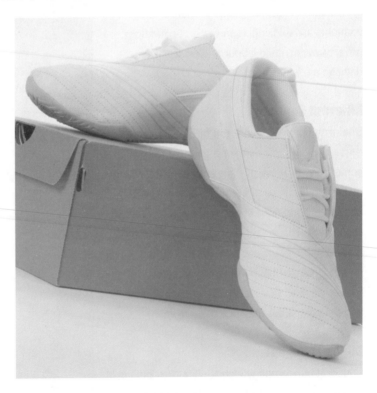

Big Brands

With the market success of fashion companies committed to ethical and sustainable fashion, many big brands in fashion are sitting up and paying attention. For example, many fashion companies and retailers in the US have joined Business for Social Responsibility, a not-for-profit organization that provides practical assistance for companies moving towards being green. Members include Levi-Strauss, Donna Karan, Liz Claiborne, Nike, Reebok and Philips-Van Heusen, as well as retailers like Sears and Wal-mart.

Natural Fibres

We have generally considered natural fibres, such as cotton, wool, silk and linen, to be good or green because they are natural. The problem is that in order to supply the world with textiles in vast quantities, farmers and growers have been constantly encouraged to increase yields. Such intensive production means the use of fertilizers, pesticides and water for irrigation, which all impact on the environment and the health of human and animal inhabitants of the growing regions. There are also issues surrounding the welfare of animals, especially in the production of wool, silk and, of course, fur.

Cotton: Thirsty Work

Successful cotton cultivation needs long periods of frost-free weather, plenty of sunshine and good rainfall – a climate that is normal in the seasonal dry tropical and subtropical homes of cotton. However, demand for cotton has meant that it is cultivated in areas with less rainfall, which means that it requires water from irrigation. As water resources get tighter, growing cotton can lead to environmental problems; Uzbekistan, where cotton is a major export, has seen great areas of desertification and salination of the soil following the tapping of the Aral Sea for irrigation.

Organic Cotton

Although it costs more to produce, organic cotton causes less of an environmental impact than conventional cotton. Organic cotton production systems replenish and maintain soil fertility, reduce the use of toxic and persistent chemicals and fertilizers, and encourage biodiversity. Many apparel companies are now using either 100 per cent organically-grown cotton, or blending varying amounts of organic and non-organic cotton in their products, so you need to look at the labels carefully.

Wonderful Wool

Wool is wonderful; it keeps you warm and is naturally absorbent, durable, non-allergenic, renewable and sustainable. However, over the years we have developed a whole range of damaging and polluting methods for producing more wool. Sheep require large areas of land for grazing; when they are confined and their pastures are overgrazed, sheep become susceptible to mange, mites, flies and lice. In the US alone, more than 6350 kilos (14,000 lbs) of dry weight pesticides were applied to sheep. The most common of these pesticides contain water-soluble, toxic organo-phosphates that are moderately toxic to humans and highly toxic to amphibians and fish. Then there are the routine doses of drugs give to sheep to guard against internal parasites, as well as the antibiotics and growth hormones in their feed.

Conventional Wool Manufacturing

The problems do not stop there; harsh scouring agents and bleaches are used to clean and lighten wool. To finish off, we throw in lots of formaldehyde, dioxins and moth-proofing chemicals and use tons of chemical dyes that frequently use heavy metals like chrome, zinc and copper in the mix.

Organic Wool: From Sheep to Store

From sheep to store, organic wool is not chemically treated. It comes from sheep that have not been treated with synthetic or harmful chemicals and benefit from grazing on pesticide-free land that is not overgrazed.

Sensuous Silk

Silk may be beloved by couturiers, but it is despised by vegans and PETA. Why? The silk worm, which produces a single fine filament, is gassed or boiled alive when it's done its job. The mulberry silkworm (*Bombyx mori*) is actually a caterpillar that cannot live without human care because they have been bred to be blind and flightless, and with underdeveloped mouths so they cannot feed. They live only for a few days in order to produce some 500 eggs. Each egg hatches in about ten days and becomes the larva – the silkworm caterpillar. For the next 35 days, the larvae eat non-stop on a diet of mulberry leaves so that their weight increases 10,000 times. When fully grown, each worm climbs a specially provided twig and starts to spin a cocoon which becomes its home for 16 days as it morphs into a moth.

Trouble Spots

This is where it gets nasty – to get out of the cocoon, the moth makes a hole by secreting an alkali fluid that dissolves the silk. Silk farmers want as much thread as possible, so they kill the worms before they turn into moths by tossing them into boiling water or a hot oven. The heat also dissolves the sticky sericin coating on the cocoon, allowing the workers to unravel the fibre gently. To make 500 g (1 lb) of silk, some 2600 silk worms must die.

Peace Silk

For those who want silk without the killing, there are some ethical options: peace silk, or vegetarian silk, is made allowing the live moth to emerge. The silken thread has been damaged and broken into smaller strands so it is spun like cotton rather than being reeled onto a spool in a continuous thread.

Ecological Linen

Probably one of the most ecologically sound fabrics, linen is woven from the fibres of the flax plant. No part of the plant is wasted; the remaining linseeds, oil, straw and fibre are used in a wide range of products including health foods, paper, oil, linoleum, soaps and cattle feed. Producing linen also uses much less water and energy than producing cotton, and linen products are biodegradable and recyclable.

Other Alternatives

In addition to the natural fibres above, there are lots of others that are being used in apparel manufacturing. Hemp is becoming increasingly popular since it requires no pesticides or herbicides, controls the erosion of topsoil and produces oxygen. Bamboo fibres and pineapple fibres are also woven into fabrics, as are soybeans and corn, but these need to be produced in closed loop systems in order to contain and capture all of the chemicals used in their production.

Greener Footprints

Being fashionably green means choosing eco-friendly footwear. Leading the way for many years has been Birkenstock, famous for its range of shoes and sandals that include vegan and vegetarian options. An increasing number of show designers and manufacturers now produce eco-friendly, organic, fair-trade, animal-free and even kosher footwear. What's more, they're comfortable and look good too!

Caring for Your Clothes

Caring for your clothes prolongs their life. This means that you can wear them for longer and, even if you do recycle them by donating them to a friend or a charity store, they will last for a long time. This keeps them out of landfill and reduces the need to produce new clothes. You can care for your clothes in numerous ways: by cleaning and ironing them carefully, by storing them well and by mending them.

Lovely Laundry

Whenever you add a new item to your wardrobe, always look at the international care labels sewn into the seam; this will give you the best advice on how to care for it. Before washing anything, sort your laundry into piles: white cottons and linens, woollens and non-colourfast items.

Laundry Tips

And to avert any laundry disasters, do the following:

- **Secure zips and fastenings**: This will stop them breaking and snagging fabric.
- **Empty pockets.**
- **Remove non-washable items**: Such as belts.
- **Turn down trouser cuffs**: So you cab brush out any loose dirt.
- **Check items for stains**: Pre-treat them.
- **Turn corduroy and textured garments inside out**: This stops them picking up fibres shed from other garments.

Ironing Tips

- **Use foil**: Reflect back more of your iron's heat by slipping some kitchen foil, shiny side upwards, under your ironing board cover.
- **Begin ironing with items that require the coolest temperature**: Then increase the heat. This saves energy, saves time waiting for the iron to cool down and avoids scorching.
- **Iron embroidered items on the reverse side**: Place a towel under the embroidery to prevent it being crushed.
- **Silk is best ironed when it's evenly damp**: Except shantung, which must be bone-dry. To prevent iron marks, put a sheet of white tissue paper between the iron and silk, then iron on a 'two dot' setting on the reverse.

Iron linen when it's quite damp: A hot iron will smooth it beautifully.

 Press woollens by placing a damp cloth over the garment: Hold the iron in place for a few seconds, then lift and move to the next spot. Don't slide the iron as you would on other garments or you'll stretch woollen ones out of shape.

In the Closet

You've taken the trouble to launder and iron your clothes, now take the same care about hanging and storing them so that, when you want to wear them, they look as good as when you put them in the closet. Don't put away freshly ironed clothes immediately, especially if you've used a steam iron or damp pressing cloth; let the garments air off a bit. Similarly, don't put a newly ironed garment on straight away; let it cool off so you don't add creases. When you come to put your clothes away, don't put them in wardrobes or drawers that are so full you have to squash them in – you'll just crease and crush them, undoing the work you've just done! If your wardrobes and drawers are bulging at the seams, perhaps it's time to stock-take and pass on the things you never wear to a charity store.

Top Tips for Storing Clothes

 Hang clothes on hangers as soon as you take them off: The warmth from your body will encourage creases to drop out.

- **Don't hang coats and jackets up by the little loops in the neck**: This pulls the shoulders out of shape. Likewise, don't hang your coat over the newel post of banisters.
- **Do up zips and remove belts**: This will keep garments in shape.
- **Repair hems and replace buttons**: Do this as soon as you can.
- **Ward off moths**: Moths attack woollen garments and natural fibres that have been mixed with synthetics. To ward off moth attack, make sure garments are clean before storing them.
- **Use natural, organic moth repellents**: Bags of lavender and small blocks of cedar wood, which you rub with sandpaper to release the natural oil, work well, as do whole cloves and citrus peel.
- **Absorb any atmospheric dampness**: By tying together some sticks of white blackboard chalk with ribbon and hanging the bunch in the wardrobe.

Dry Cleaning

Conventional dry cleaning is about as far from being green as you can get! The standard solvent used, perchloroethylene (known as 'perc'), is a central nervous system depressant and a listed hazardous air and water pollutant. Contrary to what some people think, dry cleaning doesn't extend the life of any garment; as with any type of cleaning, the process still puts wear and tear on the fabric. In most cases, garments labelled 'dry clean only' can generally be hand-washed with care, unless it's a really fancy garment covered in sequins, feathers and trimmings.

Green(ish) Dry Cleaning

If you have garments labelled dry clean only, you need to consider some green options. As alternatives to perc, there are some less toxic ways to dry clean clothes: some dry cleaners use a hydrocarbon called DF-2000, but this is also a neurotoxin and it can cause skin and eye irritation. It's also petroleum-based, so it contributes to global warming. EarthGreen is a silicone-based solvent used in modified dry cleaning machines, while liquid carbon dioxide (CO_2) is used in high-pressure cleaning machines. Liquid CO_2 is a viable alternative to chemical solvents since it is non-toxic, ecologically sound, cheap and available on a large scale. In liquid

Have You Thought Of?

Recycling the hangers you get from the dry cleaners? Take them back to the cleaners, or make use of them in the garden for supporting plants!

form, the CO_2 acts as the carrier for biodegradable soaps in much the same way that water does in a washing machine. Once the cycle is complete, the CO_2 turns back into gas form, and is captured and reused. The number of CO_2 dry cleaners is growing and soon perc use will be phased out. When you take garments to be dry cleaned, ask what method is used and actively seek out CO_2 cleaners to speed up the greening process.

Steam Clean

You could save yourself the expense of dry cleaning, and the trip to the cleaners' too, by using a steam wash and dry system. These are small hand-operated machines and most use less water and energy than a front-loading washing machine. Many second-hand and thrift stores use them to clean donated clothes before sale. Steam cleaners will freshen up clothes and remove wrinkles but won't necessarily remove stains. However, you can still remove them quite successfully using green products and keeping chemicals as a very last resort.

Repairing and Restyling

Looking after clothes keeps them in shape and ensures that you always look your best. Keeping hems fixed and buttons in place and small darns or repairs are well within most people's sewing abilities. For larger repairs, and for resizing and restyling outfits, you may need the help of a tailor or seamstress.

Ideas

Resizing garments, for example making them smaller in the waist or shortening, is a great way to make use of a second-hand outfit that's too big at the moment. Restyling, which takes a great deal of skill, can transform a dress into a skirt and jacket ensemble, alter a full skirt into a more fitted style, un-make pleats, and alter the style of collars and lapels. Some restyles can be done by the home sewer: a long-sleeved shirt with worn-out cuffs can be cut and made into short-sleeved one; a full-length skirt can be made knee-length or shorter, and even just a change of buttons can make over a garment.

Professional

For more radical restyling and for re-lining garments to give them a new lease of life, you need a professional. This is not necessarily a cheap alternative; you are paying for their knowledge, skills and time, but it is a much better and greener alternative to throwing out an outfit or buying a new one. Restyling also means that you will have an outfit that is much closer to haute-couture fashion as it will be altered to fit you, and you alone!

Sew and Sew

Be adventurous with out-of-date or worn clothes: repair, renovate or re-model them. If they're beyond all rescue then keep the fabric and make a patchwork quilt, a rag rug, a cushion or a sausage draft excluder for under the door and in the letterbox. Even old nylon tights and stockings can be used for stuffing – and for storing onions. Pop an onion in the toe, tie a knot, then add another onion. Keep going and you've got a handy string of onions; just cut one off when you need it.

New Knits for Old

Old jumpers can often be unravelled and the wool re-knitted into a new garment or just same-sized squares to make into a blanket. The sleeves of big jumpers can make cosy leggings for kids, a pull-on hat, or even a pair of slouchy socks or legwarmers for round the house. Join, or form, a 'knit-and-chat' group for inspiration.

On the Button

Keep old buttons (some are very decorative and can dress up an old garment) and zips for future use and repairs. You'll save yourself a trip to the stores and some money too!

Recycling Clothes

Unless you were the eldest or an only child, then you probably wore hand-me-downs you were younger. Today, it is very easy to buy, wear and throw away perfectly good garments, instead of passing them on. However, the amount of waste this creates, not to mention the cost, makes this practice increasingly unsustainable. Like all our valuable resources, clothes should be recycled.

Kids' Clothes

Children grow fast, so fast that they often outgrow relatively new clothes. If they're not going to be handed down to a younger sibling, then there are other ways of recycling children's garments. If your child has to wear a school uniform, there's usually a swap shop, run by fellow parents, where outgrown uniforms can be traded in for larger sizes. If there isn't a swap shop at your kid's school, then perhaps it's time to start one!

Trade with Friends

Borrowing someone else's clothes can work well, but it can be extremely annoying! However, trading clothes among friends, either for other garments or for cash, is a good way to refresh your wardrobe and recycle garments.

Get Organized

Fashion trade days are already popular with students, but they can also work between friends and work colleagues. All you need to do is organize a time and place with friends or colleagues, collect together the clean garments you want to get rid of, label them with your name, and let the trade begin!

Remember

Be reasonable when trading; a coat *is* worth a handbag when you never wear it. Don't be disappointed if you end up with some of your own stuff un-traded – remember that not everyone is the same size or shape or has the same lifestyle. If you've got un-traded clothes left, read on for some other ways of recycling them!

Clothing Exchanges

Many clothes, especially fashion garments, are rejected for wear before they are worn out in favour of the new season's look. Garment exchanges are a good way to dispose of your unwanted outfits and earn some cash too. Most garment exchanges operate on a sale or return basis: you take the garments in and if they are sold you get some cash; if not, you have to take them back.

What to Look for

Garment exchanges are a pretty good place to pick up reasonably priced clothes, and are especially good for major purchases such as suits and handbags and for 'classic' items like trenchcoats. Since the boom in designer baby and children's-wear labels, clothing exchanges are also a good way of recycling outgrown children's wear too.

Charity Stores

We all love a bargain and everyone dreams of finding that designer treasure hidden among the rails of their local charity store, so they are the first stop on many people's clothes shopping trips. They are a great place to source useful items to wear at home, at work and at parties. Even A-list celebrities in *Vogue* interviews report that their outfits come from Goodwill, Oxfam or the Red Cross shops, so what are you waiting for?

Buy and Donate

Not only can you find low-priced, wearable garments, you are also contributing to some good causes by helping the charity and helping to keep these valuable textiles out of landfill sites. Charity stores rely on the goodwill of consumers not only buying clothes, but donating them as well, so if you have garments you no longer wear, recycle them through your chosen charity store.

eBay

Everyone has a fashion skeleton in the wardrobe, an item that seemed gorgeous in the store, but that has been worn only once and is hidden away because it cost an arm and a leg! Stop beating yourself up about it and come to terms with the fact that you are never going to wear it, but that someone else just might!

Someone Will Want It

eBay is the place to sell this treasure! It's where many online clothing exchanges, dress agencies, individual collectors and museum curators look for items to go in their collections. eBay is also searched religiously by film and television costumers for period and contemporary outfits for new productions. Free your outfit from the confines of the wardrobe and let it live again – through eBay it may become a star! You could also make the ethical and honourable act of donating all or part of the proceeds of your sale to a charity.

Don't Buy It, Hire It

Hiring a morning suit for a wedding has been a solution for men for many years and, increasingly, formal wear – such as ballgowns, evening dresses, prom dresses as well as wedding and bridesmaid's dresses – is available for hire. Thanks to the Internet, the clothing rental market in women's wear has boomed and it is now possible to rent a designer outfit, or just a handbag, for that special occasion. Renting means that you don't have the expense of investing in a garment that you may not wear again. It also means that clothing is kept in circulation and made affordable to a wider market.

Beauty

If you were horrified by the harm to animals, people and the environment involved in making our clothes, then be aware that many of the commercial preparations for soaps, shampoos and cosmetics will be cocktails of chemicals including preservatives, synthetic perfumes and colourants that have been tested on animals. Once again, there is an increasing number of brands that are made purely from organic materials, have not been tested on animals, don't use animal products or are ethically sourced and produced.

Green Gods and Goddesses

No matter how much you spend on beauty and grooming products, they won't work miracles or compensate for too many late night, not enough fresh air, and the ravages of alcohol and smoking. If you want to look good, look to your lifestyle first and see what you can do to help your body look good. Once you've done that you can also make use of some simple, yet very effective, natural beauty tips. See over the page for oatmeal scrubs, herbal baths and more.

Face Sauna

Steam your face to open pores and sweat out impurities. Make a face sauna with some hot water, lemon juice and mint; cover your head and the edges of the bowl with a towel and lean over the bowl. Close your eyes and steam your face for 5 minutes if you have oily skin, or 2–3 minutes for normal or dry skin. This works for men too! If you like, try adding some of these herbs, which are famous for their therapeutic and healing properties:

 Fennel: For removing impurities.

 Rosemary: For deep cleansing.

 Lavender, rose petals, thyme or camomile: For gentle cleansing.

 Sage: For oily skins.

 Parsley: For dry or sensitive skin.

Dandelion: For older or weathered skins.

Have You Thought Of?

Going to the library and finding out more about the culinary and beneficial uses of herbs? You could then grow some in pots on your window ledge, ready for use!

Oatmeal Scrub

Make an oatmeal scrub. Oatmeal is a great exfoliator and terrific at sloughing off dead skin. Mix 30 ml (2 tablespoons) of coarse oatmeal with 5 ml (1 teaspoon) of honey and a dash of natural yoghurt and mix into a paste. Spread it on your face and neck, avoiding the delicate skin around your eyes, then massage gently with your fingertips. Let the paste dry, then rinse off with cold water. You can do this as an all-over body treatment too!

Facemasks

Facemasks are easy to make. Strawberries are astringent and will close pores and tighten the skin. Just mash two or three, spread them on your face, relax for 10 minutes and rinse off. Yoghurt and fuller's earth (a mineral-rich, fine grey powder, derived from single-cell algae found on the sea bed) mixed into a paste is good for oily skins. A yoghurt and pear mix is nourishing to the skin, or use up an over-ripe avocado by mashing it with a squeeze of lemon and the beaten white of an egg. Let this dry on your face, then rinse off with cool water.

Herbal Baths

As a special treat, run yourself a herbal bath. Make a muslin bag and fill it with herbs of your choice, then dangle it from the hot tap or showerhead. Instead of a body bath, you could relax and treat your feet with a herbal footbath.

 Healing herbs: Calendula, comfrey, spearmint and yarrow.

 Relaxing herbs: Camomile, jasmine, hops, valerian, meadowsweet and lime flowers.

 Stimulating and invigorating herbs: Basil, bay, fennel, eucalyptus, lavender, lemon balm, lemon verbena, mint, pine, rosemary, sage and thyme.

Crowning Glory

Nearly every shampoo today seems to contain essences of fruit, flowers or herbs. In commercial, non-organic products these are likely to be chemically synthesized versions. But you don't even have to buy organic preparations – just make them yourself! Put one application of organic baby shampoo into a cup, add four drops of essential oil and mix together thoroughly.

 For dry hair: Try essential oil of sage.

 For greasy hair: Lavender or peppermint.

 To prevent dandruff: Use camomile, rosemary or thyme.

Top Tips for Beautiful Hair

- **Protein treatment**: Sun-damaged, dried-out, bleach-damaged or brittle hair can do with a protein treatment. Whisk 3 whole eggs and 15 ml (1 tablespoon) of cider vinegar, apply to damp, clean hair, leave it on for 15 minutes, then rinse off in cold water.
- **Cider vinegar**: This makes a great tonic for greasy hair and restores the pH balance – just add a generous dash to your rinse water.
- **Rosemary**: This is a treat for normal hair: steep 3–4 springs of rosemary in a jug of boiling water for 1 hour. Strain the liquid and use for a final rinse.
- **Cool water**: If the water you use for your final rinse is cool rather than warm, it will encourage each hair's outer sheath cells to lie flat, giving your hair a smooth, shiny finish.
- **Coconut oil and olive oil**: These have for years been used as deep treatments for hair. You can also make your own herbal hair oil by adding six drops of essential oil suited to your hair type (see page 175) to 30 ml (2 tablespoons) of almond or sunflower oil. Massage the mix into your hair and scalp, wrap a hot damp towel around your head and leave it for 30 minutes (replacing the hot damp towel as required). Then wash off and rinse.

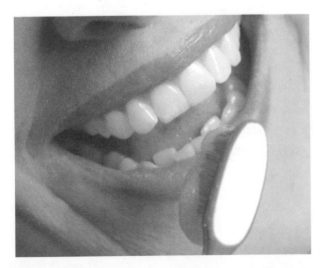

Pearly Whites

Going green will give you a lot to smile about, so make sure those pearly whites are kept well away from commercial toothpastes that contain detergents, abrasives, artificial sweeteners and chemical optical brighteners. Health food stores stock a wide range of terrific oral care products, so make these your number one choice.

Fresh Alternatives

Did you know that you can use the following?

- **A fresh sage leaf**: Rubbed over your teeth and gums, this is an effective cleaner.
- **DIY toothpaste**: A paste made of 5 ml (1 teaspoon) of bicarbonate of soda, two drops of essential oil of peppermint and a little water makes a very effective toothpaste.
- **A strawberry**: Rubbed over your teeth removes tea and coffee stains.
- **Fresh parsley or watercress**: Both high in chlorophyll, the main ingredient in most mouthwashes, and make breath fresheners when chewed.
- **Cardamom**: For garlicky breath, chew a cardamom seed and its husk.

Checklist

- **Be a conscious consumer**: Buy what you *need*, not what you want.
- **Buy ethically produced and organic goods**: Wherever possible.
- **Use the Internet**: Search out companies, products and suppliers who are actively working towards green principles.
- **Look after your wardrobe**: Carefully clean, iron and store your clothes.
- **Repair and reuse your existing wardrobe**: By mending or tailoring clothes.
- **Recycle clothes you never wear**: Consider donating to charity, swapping with friends or selling on eBay.
- **Look at natural beauty products**: And avoid the cocktail of chemicals that may have been tested on animals.

Celebrations

Gifts for All Occasions

Whatever the occasion – birthdays, anniversaries, weddings, Christmas and all the other big days of the year – celebrate them by going green. There are numerous, simple ways in which this can be done without having to give up any of the fun elements of the day, such as exchanging gifts. All you have to do is remember the green tenets of reduce, reuse and recycle, then perhaps consider some of the ideas in this chapter.

Giving Gifts

When we buy gifts for friends or family, we often choose things that we would, in fact, like for ourselves. Consequently, such gifts may not be useful or to the recipient's taste. How many times have you given, or received, a present that gets hidden away for a while until it's thrown out? This is a waste of resources and the item will more than likely end up in a landfill site. Giving a green gift solves the perennial problem of 'what do I get this person', and at the same time you give a gift that lasts.

Green Gifts

The act of giving doesn't necessarily involve buying something; some of the nicest gifts are literally green – ones that you have grown. A pot of herbs, some flowers from your garden or cuttings from a plant are all heartfelt gifts that will be warmly received.

Alternative Gifts

Give a gift that says you not only care about the recipient, but also about the planet and the people on it. Alternative gifts come in a range of forms and many green or ethical groups, as well as charities, now have great gift ideas: www.greatgifts.org, www.oxfamunwrapped.com, www.gifts4life.com and www.goodgifts.org are just a few that can be found online. From these, and others, it's possible to give a gift which is in fact a donation to a good cause. Some of the most popular alternative gifts include:

- **Livestock**: Such as goats, cows, water buffalo, chickens, ducks and bees to help farmers in developing countries.
- **Football team sponsorship**: For street children around the world.
- **Mobile health clinics.**
- **Wells and clean water supplies.**
- **Immunization programmes**: And treatment for HIV/AIDS and TB.
- **Education and training**: For health workers and midwives.
- **School equipment and books.**
- **Micro-loans**: For fish farmers and female entrepreneurs.
- **Tree sponsorship**: A tree is planted, or ancient woodland maintained, as your gift.

Use the Internet

In most instances, you choose the amount you wish to spend, the money is allocated to a gift and your recipient receives a card or notification. Search the Internet for different organizations and match them and their gift offerings to the personality or convictions of the person you are buying a gift for.

Sustainable and Fairtrade Gifts

When you buy someone, or yourself, a gift, make sure that you choose products that are made out of sustainably grown and managed materials; for example, wooden toys that are marked with the FSC (Forest Stewardship Council) logo. Fairtrade products range from clothes and jewellery to chocolate and flowers, so whatever you decide to buy, chances are you can guarantee your gift is green.

Recycled Gifts

Great gifts don't always have to be new. Show that you know the recipient's tastes in literature and music by getting them a second-hand book or record that you know they will love. Antiques, collectibles and jewellery often become treasured presents – with no thought given to the fact that they are second-hand. Buying antique or old jewellery is a good way to recycle precious metals and gemstones, and it means that you aren't adding to the earth's problems caused by mining.

Vouchers

When you really want to give a tangible present but are short on ideas, gift vouchers work a treat as they let the recipient choose exactly what they want. Many of the green shopping sites – both retail and online – offer this service and products range from the familiar book tokens and music vouchers to organic food and drink hampers and gardening goods.

Favours

Favours are another way of giving, where you offer a service: anything from a back rub to babysitting or a month's worth of washing-up! These are great gifts for kids to give; they cost nothing, do not harm the environment and are negotiable!

Sign Them Up

If a friend or relative has a particular interest, why not think of a gift that enables them to pursue it further? Sign them up for a series of yoga classes, a bird-watching trip or a cycle maintenance course. Paying for them to become a member of a national conservation organization would mean that they could enjoy getting out and about while also contributing to the maintenance and preservation of natural and historic sites. Alternatively, if they're culture vultures, give them theatre or concert tickets, or make a donation in their name so they become friends of a museum, art gallery or theatre. A subscription to their favourite journal – which could be online – would also be an appreciated gift.

Wrapping Up

There's no real need for presents to be wrapped up – especially if they're already packaged. However, we are used to giving and receiving gifts that are beautifully wrapped and unfortunately the paper usually ends up in a waste mountain.

Reused Paper

When you receive a present, don't just keep the gift – save the paper and use it to wrap presents for other people.

Recycled Paper

If you must wrap, choose recycled paper: the World Wildlife Fund has a great selection on its website. Brown paper always looks interesting tied with string; both parts are reusable and there's always an interesting and thoughtful gift inside!

Tissue Paper

Another green choice would be tissue paper; plain white looks chic and can be reused for wrapping up summer clothes for winter storage.

Make Your Own

There's no reason why you can't make your own wrapping paper. You could cut out and collage magazine images onto sheets of newspaper. Alternatively, why not wrap one gift in another: a fair-traded silk scarf makes beautiful 'paper'. Likewise, make a gift tag. These don't have to be paper: try a pressed flower or a pinecone tied with a ribbon. The only limitations are in your imagination!

Have You Thought Of?

Making your own wrapping paper and greetings cards by reusing scrap materials? Personalize these and people will be touched by the time and effort you have spent.

Greetings Cards

Cards can be problematic; while there's always something magical about receiving a card in the mail, their manufacture involves a great deal of cutting down trees and chemical processes to transform the pulp into paper.

E-cards

The first green solution is to send fewer paper cards and send e-cards instead. You can either make your own by uploading a festive photograph, or go to a specialist site that provides e-cards for all occasions. They'll even send them out for you as well!

Green Cards

Green cards are compostable or biodegradable cards that you plant back into the earth as they contain the seed of a tree or wildflower.

Charity Cards

Charity cards at Christmas are a way of offsetting some of the excess of the season with a donation to a good cause. Make sure you buy charity cards at charity stores or at their own charity stalls at fetes – this way around 80 per cent of the proceeds will actually go to the charity. High-street stores selling charity cards often hand over as little as five per cent of the retail price to the charity.

Recycle

Don't forget to compost your cards where possible; unfortunately, glittery and heavily glossed cards aren't suitable. At Christmas time, you can put them in the card recycling bins that are set up at some supermarkets.

Party Time

Each year the calendar offers us a host of celebrations: birthdays, seasonal and religious festivals, and once-in-a-lifetime events, such as weddings, that call for a special party. Whatever the day, knowing that everyone had a good time is important, but making sure it doesn't cost the earth can make it even more memorable. Follow your green principles and make every celebration from Easter to Mother's Day doubly significant.

Party Food: Use your LOAF

Celebrations involve eating and drinking so use your LOAF when it comes to food and drink. LOAF stands for Local, Organic, Animal Friendly and Fairtrade. If you stick to these principles when in the supermarket, you can't go wrong. Consider waste – don't buy or cook more than you need. Some children's party foods can be a problem; full of sugar, E-numbers, artificial colours and preservatives, they transform little angels into shrieking monsters of hyperactivity. While once-in-a-while treats won't hurt them, wherever possible, try to provide healthy, tasty and organic foods. And if you're using paper plates, make sure they are biodegradable. See the chapter Food & Drink, pages 124–153, for more information.

Be My Green Valentine

Valentine's Day is easily dismissed by cynics as a day invented for the sole purpose of buying cliché-ridden gifts of roses and heart-shaped boxes of chocolates. However, you can be sentimental and eco-conscious at the same time. Forget red hearts, Valentine's Day is the perfect excuse to show your love with a green gift.

Chocolates

These are possibly the most widely bought items on Valentine's Day – make sure yours are organic and fairly traded. Organic chocolate is widely available in supermarkets now so there's no excuse not to make this your first choice. Brands including Booja Booja, Go Raw and XOX offer vegan chocolates, and fairtrade brands such as Divine and Theo also offer a range of green chocolates.

Roses

To accompany the chocolates, a dozen long-stemmed red roses are traditional but not necessarily sustainable, depending on where the roses have come from and how they have been grown. Make sure your gift shows love for the planet as well as for your intended by buying organic, pesticide-free flowers. One eco-label to look out for is VeriFlora; this ensures that the flowers are grown to strict environmental and social sustainability standards. Roses don't have to be the only green gift; why not choose a bunch of local, seasonal flowers? Or give a windowsill herb garden, some potted bulbs or a sapling? Like your love, these will carry on growing.

Green Unions

If Valentine's Day went according to plan and you and your true love are planning to tie the knot, then there's a lot of organizing to do. When you start to plan, keep your green principles to the fore – the wedding invitations, the gown, the cake and the flowers can all be green.

Green the Rings

You may not decide to have your wedding rings fashioned out of hemp, but you do have a few green options:

- ☑ **Recycled**: Look at buying recycled gold, silver or platinum.
- ☑ **Avoid 'blood diamonds'**: Opt for certificated conflict-free stones. A reputable jeweller should be able to tell you exactly where the diamonds came from.
- ☑ **Select antique or vintage rings**: They can be resized if too small or too big.

The Bride Wore...Green!

Green grooms might go for the rental option, but brides generally want a dress of their own. This doesn't mean that there aren't beautiful vintage gowns out there waiting to go down the aisle again.

If you want something new, then there are some beautiful dresses made from hemp, organic cotton, bamboo- and soy-based textiles and peace silk.

Donate a Dress

It is the dream of many Liberian brides to be married in white, but in a land ravaged by war and where wages are often less than 75p ($1) a day, the dream is all too often out of reach. Liberian Ambassador Alpha Bird Collins and his wife Louise launched the Liberian Wedding Dress Project following their own wedding. You can donate your own dress to the project; it is then loaned out to Liberian brides for a small charge (to cover cleaning). Men's suits and bridesmaids' outfits are also welcome. Don't forget that your own local charity store would also be happy to recycle your dress.

The Bouquet

This, naturally, should be organic, but you might also think about locally grown and seasonal blooms for your bouquet. If you're planning on preserving the flowers after the wedding –

even some of the greenest brides might balk at the idea of composting their bouquet – then the eco-friendly way to do it is by pressing them, since freeze-drying requires the use of harmful chemicals.

Finishing Touches

There's so much to consider when you plan your wedding or civil ceremony that some things might get overlooked. Here are some green tips for making a big difference on your big day:

 Look for Fairtrade and recycled stationery products: Or send e-invites with an RSVP button for instant responses!

 Make your cake organic: With Fairtrade and free-range ingredients.

Make your own confetti: You can do this using recycled paper or locally produced flower petals. Or how about bird-friendly seeds? Don't use rice though, as it's a waste of a valuable food and the birds can't eat it.

Go for green transport: Hire a LPG or electric car to get you to the church on time or, for the real romantics, a horse-drawn carriage. Get guests to car-pool and share their journeys, or hire a bus to take them from a single collection point to the venue.

Use local catering companies: Look for ones who can provide organic, locally sourced, or Fairtrade food and wines.

Make your wedding pictures digital: Save paper and chemicals by making your photographs available for friends and family to view online.

Ask for green gifts: Or sign up to one of the aid-giving lists so your guests can donate to your choice of ethical or green causes.

Go on an eco-friendly honeymoon: For more on green travel, see the chapter Getting Away pages 214–229.

Have You Thought Of?

Planting a tree to commemorate a significant event?

Ecological Easter

Easter is one of the most important religious feasts of the Christian calendar, but it has become so commercialized into an excess of spending, eating and waste that many are tempted to ignore it. This would be a shame, as the season marks a spirit of renewed hope and optimism. So, whether you celebrate the religious significance of Easter or not, there are ways to make the event greener, healthier and more meaningful. For example, Kenyan Nobel Peace Prize winner Wangari Maathai has called on people around the world to plant a tree at Easter as a symbol of renewal and to help protect the planet.

Green Eggs

Eggs have been used in spring festivals since ancient Greek and Roman times, as symbols of the new birth of the land after the dark days of winter. The tradition of giving chocolate eggs to mark the end of the Lent fast dates back to the nineteenth century. If you do indulge, make sure that the chocolate you buy is organic and fairly traded; that way, you'll guarantee a fair price for the raw materials and ensure that there are no added chemicals, preservatives or synthetic colours. Choose eggs that have minimal wrapping and then make sure that this is recycled or composted.

Blow Your Own

A fun Easter activity for kids is to decorate their own hens' eggs (free range and organic, of course). You can either hardboil an egg, or pierce the shell of a raw egg at both ends with a pin and blow hard through one of the holes to expel the contents. Then use organic, plant-based food colourings as paints; if you mix 1 tsp of vinegar with a few drops of food colouring, the vinegar will keep the colours bright and streak-free. Alternatively, have fun experimenting with your own homemade vegetable dyes: brown onion skins steeped in boiling water produce a yellow dye; red cabbage makes a blue dye; and beetroot juice makes a great pink.

Bunnies and Bilbies

The symbol of the Easter rabbit dates back to the second century in Europe when the Saxon fertility goddess Eastre was symbolized by a hare. Do resist the temptation of bringing home a live rabbit at Easter, unless you are prepared to care for it for the rest of its life. If you are, then check out your local humane society or animal rescue centre and re-home an animal in need. In Australia, where keeping rabbits is illegal in many states, you could sponsor a bilby instead; these marsupials are in danger of extinction due to loss of habitat.

Merry Green Christmas

Although Christmas is the season of joy and goodwill, it can also be a time of huge waste and consumption. However, it is possible to have a merry, green Christmas by putting a bit of consideration into the way you celebrate.

Evergreen Tree

Instead of buying a Christmas tree, consider decorating a houseplant instead – with a few decorations, it will look just as festive. Although artificial trees may sound like a good idea, since they last for a number of years, in reality real trees are more eco-friendly. This is because artificial trees require a lot of energy to make, are often imported from overseas and can end up in a landfill site where they do not biodegrade. When buying a real tree, make sure that you are happy with its source; it should ideally that it comes from a local, small-scale, sustainable grower. Instead of a cut tree, why not consider a tree with a root ball, which can be planted out in the garden in the New Year? If you do have a cut tree, make sure that after Twelfth Night, you dispose of it responsibly by sending it to the compost heap or taking it to a tree-recycling centre.

Lights

Consider LEDs instead of incandescent lights to decorate the tree. Although these are more expensive to buy, they last much longer and use 80–90 per cent less power. And don't let your energy saving principles go out of the window just because it's Christmas. As with any light in the house, don't have the Christmas tree lights blazing away unless you are there to enjoy them – switch them off at night to be safe and save energy.

Decorations

Decorating the house at Christmas is one of the things that makes the season so special. There are many environmentally friendly ways to do this:

- **Holly and ivy**: Decorate your home in the traditional way – with holly and ivy. Do respect Mother Nature though and only take what you need. Once the Christmas period is over, don't forget to put it in the compost bin.
- **Make your own decorations**: Get creative using recycled and scrap materials.
- **Fairtrade**: If you do buy decorations, look for fair-trade items that are interesting, hand-crafted objects of great beauty that you will want to get out year after year.

Checklist

- **Remember the three Rs**: Reduce, reuse and recycle.
- **Buy local, organic and fair-trade**: Including food and presents.
- **Make a donation**: Donate to charities and aid organisations in lieu of personal gifts.
- **Cut down on waste**: By reusing paper and sending e-cards.
- **Donate your dress**: Consider donating your wedding dress to a charity.
- **Think about packaging**: Buy Easter eggs with the least amount of packaging or paint your own.
- **Don't buy an artificial Christmas tree**: Either decorate a houseplant or buy a tree from a local, sustainable source.

Getting Around

The Need For Carbon Neutral Transport

Transport is a major issue that concerns individuals, local and national government. Most people only become concerned about green transport when oil prices rise; when prices drop, they forget all about it. Regardless of the price of oil, we need to remember that it is not an infinite resource and take into account the damage being inflicted on the environment from greenhouse gas emissions and oil spills. We must also consider the manufacturing and production problems associated with cars, including the disposal of old vehicles and products such as tyres.

CO$_2$ Emissions

Much of the current debate about transport centres on CO_2 emissions, since the gas contributes to climate change. Every gallon of petrol/gasoline used results in about 9 kg/20 lbs of CO_2 being produced. Most of the weight of the CO_2 emitted doesn't come from the fuel itself, but from the oxygen in the air that is burned in the combustion process; the chemical reactions between the fuel and oxygen produce CO_2. While it is possible to use carbon credits to offset your carbon footprint, this doesn't tackle the source of the problem.

Other Polluting Emissions

Unfortunately, CO_2 is not the only thing emitted form the exhausts of petrol/diesel-powered vehicles. The following pollutants are also produced and have a significant impact on the environment and health:

- **Carbon monoxide**: Odourless and tasteless, yet highly toxic, it reduces the body's ability to handle oxygen. Carbon monoxide occurs naturally in our atmosphere at around 0.1 ppm (parts per million) – car exhausts without a catalytic converter contain around 7,000 ppm.
- **Nitrogen oxides**: A major contributor to smog that can cause long-term health problems.
- **Benzene**: A known carcinogen in humans. It is also toxic to aquatic life and can cause death in plants.
- **Sulphur dioxide**: A contributor to acid rain. It can also cause pulmonary and respiratory problems.
- **Formaldehyde**: Another known carcinogen for humans, with many similar effects for animals and birds.
- **Particulate matter**: The soot, or the particles of dust, debris and metals, can be inhaled and increase the likelihood of blood clots.

Green Alternatives

It is unlikely that technology will ever deliver us a fuel that is completely non-polluting, and even a bicycle isn't truly green if you take into account its materials and manufacture. However, we can all take green steps towards minimizing the impact of our actions on the planet and help to save the dwindling resources we have. Making some small changes to our lifestyle and habits can help a great deal – and there are a number of added benefits, such as saving money and increasing fitness!

On Foot

Too often the car is the default transport mode for even the shortest journeys. Paradoxically, some even drive their cars to the gym. If you can, make short journeys on foot, or incorporate a walk as part of your regular commute. Many will argue that while they can get to the shops or to the station, they can't carry everything they need. The solution: get a trolley on wheels. This will take the weight off your arms and let you step out in style. For winter or late nights, pack a high-visibility vest so you can be seen.

On Your Bike

Bikes are very efficient modes of transport, and there's a bike out there to suit everyone – from adventurous mountain bikes to lightweight racing cycles and fold-up commuter models. You can even get recycled bikes, bikes made from bamboo and hybrid bikes, which are part pedal-powered, part electric. Bikes last a long time, take comparatively little maintenance and, if you use your common sense, are pretty safe too. Do wear a cycle helmet, get some good lights and a high-visibility vest, and make use of cycle lanes and routes.

Don't Be Put Off

Although there are a couple of drawbacks to cycling, don't let these put you off:

- **The weather**: A cold, rainy day can be off-putting. However, with a good set of waterproofs to go over your clothes you shouldn't get too wet!
- **Storage**: This can be a particular problem for flat/apartment dwellers, as most communal hallways must be kept clear for emergency access. A folding bike, or a lightweight bike and hanging rack, might be worth considering – better than chaining it up outside where it can be stolen. If several of your work colleagues cycle in, lobby your employer for secure bike parking.
- **Punctures**: These inevitably occur. A short cycle maintenance course will show you how to fix them quickly. There are also different types of tyres to choose from, which could reduce the number of punctures you have.
- **Once you've cycled, walking feels really slow**: On the plus side, it's free, it's good exercise and you get out and about – especially as many cycle routes take riders away from busy roads. The popularity of cycling has encouraged many cities to introduce free or short-term bike rental schemes to get about town.

Accessorize

The low-impact, low-tech bike is perfectly suited to our high-tech world: you can get a hands-free mobile phone holder for the handle bars, and whiz kids can even use their pedal power to charge up batteries for mobile devices. A bike trailer or panniers will carry everything you need for a day at the office and you can even get a DoggyRide for pooches that need to take a break from walkies.

Public Transport

For long distances and commuting, public transport is most people's only option – and often the bane of their life! It's not the journey itself that gets people down, or the distance, but the time it takes and the unrelenting routine. Nevertheless, making a switch from car to public transport makes green, and often economic, sense. Not only does someone else have to shoulder the responsibility of driving, you can also make use of the journey time to read, surf the net, text message or just look at the scenery.

Scoot Off on a Scooter

Increasingly popular around towns and cities are scooters. Scooters are easy to drive since the controls are minimal and many have automatic gear changing. They are also inexpensive to run: the tank of an average scooter holds about 1–2 gallons (4–9 litres) and most modern scooters do more than 50 mpg (80 km/g), with many reaching 100 mpg (160 km/g) – that's three or four times more efficient than the average car.

Electric

If your commute allows it, and you can recharge it easily, you could opt for an electric scooter with no emissions. Like electric cars, electric scooters have a lower top speed and a more limited range than petrol-powered ones – but then, how fast can you really go during rush hour?

Safety

You must always wear a helmet. Furthermore, while in some places a car driver's licence is not required, if you are considering buying a scooter, make sure you get some training – and make sure you know your highway code. Follow some of the green driving tips (see page 207), and you might save even more money.

Wedded to the Wheel

In some instances, the car is the only viable transport option available. Even so, there are still lots of ways in which drivers can lessen their impact on the environment and reduce their carbon footprint. They range from the very simple, such as making sure your tyres are correctly inflated, to more complicated decisions about types of cars and their fuels.

To Start With

There are ways to lessen your environmental impact when in the car:

- **One trip, multiple jobs**: Consider planning on doing as many jobs as possible in one car trip – five jobs in one trip is better than five separate journeys.
- **Avoid rush hour**: Where possible, avoid travelling at peak or rush hours where congestion means delays. Leave earlier or later to avoid traffic.
- **Switch off**: When you're stuck in a traffic jam, your car is doing zero miles to the gallon, so switch the engine off.
- **Reduce noise**: Environmental pollution comes in many forms, one of which is noise. Turn your car stereo down, get your screaming clutch and noisy exhaust (tailpipe) fixed and make sure your car alarm isn't going off at 3 am.

Swim in the Car Pool

Car pool or shared journeys emerged out of the first oil crisis in the 1970s. They're a very good idea and work well, especially as the crisis we face today is much greater. Car-sharing sites on the web will list geographic options, matching departure and destination routes, as well as chronological options, matching times of departure and arrival. In the USA and Canada, check out www.erideshare.com and www.carpoolconnect.com; in Australia, try www.thecarpool.com; in the UK and Europe, check out www.liftshare.com and www.carshare.com.

School Run

Car sharing is ideal for journeys like the school run. You could organize a roster of parents so one car takes four children rather than four cars being on the road. If you don't own a car, you can still join in and share costs.

Buying a Car

If you're going to buy a car, buy a recycled one – a nearly-new car. That way it will be as up to date as possible with regards to emissions, possibly still under the manufacturer's warranty and any repairs that do need to be made will be cheaper. Size matters, too – buy as small a car as you can for your everyday needs. A big car may be impressive, but if most of your driving is done within an 80 km (50 mile) radius of your home, then a big car may turn out to be very expensive and very inefficient to run. You can always rent a bigger car for longer journeys.

Buying a Fuel-efficient Car

If you are in the market for a car, make your choice based on its fuel efficiency. The fuel economy of similar-sized cars can vary by as much as 45 per cent, so do some homework first!

Fuel

The next thing to consider is the type of fuel your car is going to run on: petrol, diesel, biofuels, electricity, LPG (Liquefied Petroleum Gas or Auto Gas), or a hybrid car, beloved of green celebrities.

What's Biofuel?

Biofuels are fuels derived from organic matter, either animal or vegetable. It's not a new idea; Henry Ford's famous Model T, produced in 1908, was designed to run on ethanol, and Rudolph Diesel's demonstration engine in 1912 ran on peanut oil, but, as cheap petroleum-based fuels took over, biofuels went onto the back burner.

Benefits of Biofuels

 A renewable source.

 Absorb CO_2: The plants grown to make biofuels absorb the same amount of CO_2 as is released when the fuel is burned, making for significantly lower emissions than fossil fuels.

Disadvantages of Biofuels

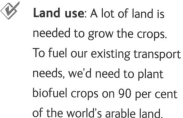

 Land use: A lot of land is needed to grow the crops. To fuel our existing transport needs, we'd need to plant biofuel crops on 90 per cent of the world's arable land.

 Rainforest clearance: The demand for biofuels puts pressure on the world's rainforests, as they are cleared for biofuel crop growing. This could mean that the net loss in carbon capture by bio diesel crops. compared to the rainforests. would result in a far greater impact on global warming.

 Engine modification: Most cars will run on biofuels but only after engine modification, which in many cases makes the manufacturer's warranties null and void.

 Refuelling outlets: These are still very thin on the ground.

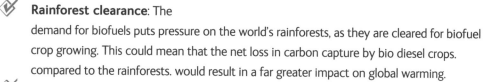

Liquefied Petroleum Gas: Auto Gas

LPG, or Auto Gas, is a mix of butane and propane, and is produced in the refinement of crude oil or, in some cases, extracted from oil or natural gas seams. While it's still basically a fossil fuel, it's a little greener than petrol or diesel as it generates 15 per cent less CO_2 and 20 per cent fewer of the other deadly emissions when combusted. It also evaporates quickly if spilled, so there's no risk to water or soil contamination. Very few motor manufacturers offer LPG versions of their vehicles so most cars have to be converted to run on LPG. This is expensive – you'd have to keep the car for a long time to recoup the financial savings. However, in a great green step, Australia has recently announced a subsidy for LPG conversions.

All-electric Cars

Electric cars have become a familiar sight in many of our cities over the past decade. These are propelled by electric motors and, unlike other electric vehicles (like trams or electric trains), need a battery from which they get all their power. The battery is recharged as needed from an external source – i.e. you plug it in! If you use the car in the city, but have a garage or off-road space in which to recharge the battery overnight, then an all-electric car can make sense.

Benefits of All-electric Cars

- **Greenest option**: All-electric cars are the greenest option, especially if the electricity they use comes from renewable sources.
- **Zero emissions from the car**: This makes cities greener places to live.
- **Cost**: They're very cheap to run and to maintain.
- **Taxes**: In some cities and countries, all-electric vehicles are exempt from congestion charges and/or road taxes and duties.

Disadvantages of All-electric Cars

- **Not *very* fast**: Generally, they have a lower top speed than conventional cars – although they can still be pretty quick.

Size: They are smaller than conventional cars, which makes them unsuited to families.

 Distance: They are limited in the distance they can travel between recharges, so are not suited to long journeys.

 Charging points: The are not yet many public charging points.

Pollution problems: There are potential pollution problems when it comes to disposing of the batteries.

Hybrid Cars

A hybrid car uses electricity alongside petrol or diesel fuel. Hybrid cars have the power to their transmission provided from a battery by means of an electric motor. The conventionally fuelled engine recharges the battery and supplies extra power to the transmission. This means that hybrid cars have a higher top speed than all-electric vehicles and there's no need to plug them into the mains to recharge the batteries.

Advantages of Hybrids

 Fuel-efficient: Hybrid cars are about 50 per cent more fuel-efficient than a conventional vehicle; the engine is recharging the batteries at times when that energy would usually be wasted, such as at traffic lights.

 Fewer emissions: Increased efficiency means fewer emissions and cheaper fuel costs.

 Taxes: Like all-electric vehicles, in some cities hybrids are exempt from paying congestion charges and/or road taxes and duties.

 You can drive as normal: Hybrids are capable of making long journeys.

Disadvantages of Hybrids

 Fossil fuels: Hybrids still rely on fossil fuels and therefore still generate greenhouse gases.

 Cost: They have a higher purchase price and the cost of replacing worn-out batteries is high.

 Limited choice: The range of vehicles is limited to large saloons; manufacturers seem intent on having top-speed models to match conventional cars rather than producing an extended range of small hybrid hatchbacks or super-minis.

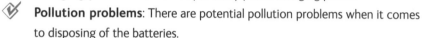

Green Driving

> If you need to have a car, and an electric, LPG or hybrid version is out of the question, in addition to cutting journeys and car-sharing, the way you drive can reduce the impact your car has on the environment. Greener driving may simply mean changing some of those long-held bad driving habits.

Ready for the Off?

Paying a little bit of attention to your vehicle before you set off on a journey can help both save money and reduce pollution. Then, once you're on the road, a few simple changes to your existing driving style will make a big difference to the planet.

Green Journey Tips

Before you leave, check the following:

- **Reduce weight and fuel consumption**: Do this by taking unnecessary items out of your car. These include tools, sports equipment, walking boots.... Leave behind anything that's not needed on that journey.
- **Remove roof racks and roof storage boxes**: There is no point in having these attached to your car when they are not needed, and the wind resistance they create dramatically increases fuel consumption.
- **Make sure your tyres are inflated to the correct pressure**: For safety's sake and for fuel economy. For every 6 psi the tyre is under-inflated, fuel consumption increases by one per cent.

Avoid overfilling the tank: Spilled fuel evaporates and releases harmful emissions.

 Keep your engine tuned: Like a piano, a car engine needs tuning for it to hit the right notes and make it fuel-efficient.

Keep your air filters clean: A clean air filter can save you as much as 15 per cent in fuel costs. Old, worn or dirty filters allow dirt into the engine, which not only affects the fuel consumption, but can also lead to more expensive engine faults. Think of the engine as a heart, and dirty air filters as clogged-up arteries.

 Use good-quality engine oil: Engine oil is there to reduce friction, and less friction means less fuel is used. Make sure you use the right grade of oil for your engine or you'll cause overheating and wear problems.

HAVE YOU THOUGHT OF?

Planning your route?
Nothing wastes more fuel than getting lost!

Green Driving Tips

Once you're on your way, bear these driving tips in mind:

Drive with the windows up: At speeds of 40 mph (64 km/h), drive with the windows up – this reduces drag and improves fuel efficiency.

Limit the air conditioning use: Only use air conditioning on really hot days, as it uses up fuel.

Switch off the engine: If you think you are going to be stationary for more than two minutes, for example in traffic jams or at level crossings, switch off the engine.

Drive sedately and think ahead: This allows you to moderate your speed, avoid sharp braking (thereby saving fuel) and join traffic smoothly.

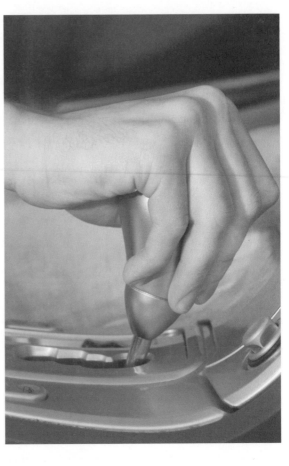

 Keep your speed down: Driving at 50–55 mph (80–88 km/h) means your car is running at optimum fuel efficiency and is producing fewer emissions. But be aware, 15 mph (24 km/h) is the most polluting speed.

 Drive in the right gear: Staying in the upper rev range in each gear for long periods consumes vast amounts of fuel.

 Avoid harsh acceleration and sudden braking: These can use up to 30 per cent more fuel and increase the wear and tear on tyres and the engine.

 Select your music beats with care: We respond to the rhythms and speed of music – which is why marching bands march, yoga classes are calm and aerobics classes 'pump it up'. Fast-paced and loud music makes you drive faster than you need to.

 Reduce the use of accessories: Any accessories powered by electricity will impact on your fuel use. Air conditioning, heaters (unless it's air heated by the engine), stereos, headlights and heated seats all use fuel.

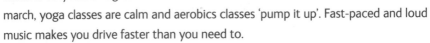 **Accelerate before a hill**: When you meet a hill, it's more fuel-efficient to accelerate before it than on it.

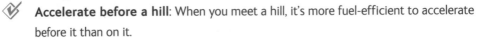

Greener Tyres

We often think the tyres we put on our cars are made of rubber, a renewable resource, when in fact over 90 per cent of all tyres are made from synthetic materials. Their production and disposal are major environmental problems: the illegal dumping of tyres by the roadside or in rivers is an all-too-often visible reminder of this.

Toxic Tyres

One dumped tyre leads to another – or three! And soon they grow into huge piles that, when set alight, create a noxious cocktail of fumes. The run-off from melted residues and the water used to extinguish the fires can also contaminate the soil and the groundwater. Burning tyres alongside other types of fuel such as coal has long been used as a method of disposal (and generating electricity), but such disposal adds to air pollution and means increased amounts of heavy metals deposited in the environment. Taking tyres to a recycling centre may sound like a good idea, but in truth around 25 per cent of these tyres end up being burned, so check with the tyre centre where they will end up.

Tyres That Go Round and Round

Tyres are a necessary evil, but there are ways in which we can reduce the numbers being disposed of dangerously, and save some money too.

Retreaded or Recapped

Retreaded/recapped or remoulded tyres offer one way to keep tyres out of landfill sites and stop them being burned. A retreaded or recapped tyre is one where an already cured and embossed ribbon of tyre tread material is applied with an adhesive to a prepared casing and cured in an autoclave tyre chamber. The casing is usually an old worn tyre that has had its old tread removed.

Remoulded

A remoulded or remanufactured tyre is essentially the same, except that it usually has a new veneer added to the sidewalls, which is sometimes called 'bead-to-bead' retreading. These are high-quality tyres with no compromise on safety or road handling. However, it is important that consumers insist that a reputable retreader has processed them and that they carry a warranty at least as good as a new tyre.

Green Diamond Tires

A development in the USA by Green Diamond Tires (GDT) remoulds tyres by embedding thousands of silicon carbide (industrial diamond) granules throughout the depth of the tread. Not only will these tyres last 45,000 miles (72,000 km), they also require less fuel in their production, are all-weather tyres, and all manufacturing by-products are recycled into other products such as road substrate, decking, fencing, and playground or athletic track material.

Recycled

Tyres are recyclable – and not just into other tyres. Recycling specialist retailers and online stores have a huge selection of really useful items all made from recycled tyres, ranging from pens, notebooks and mouse mats to window boxes and planters, belts and sandals. You can even get your shoes or boots resoled with recycled tyre. On a more specialist level, recycled tyre is also used in insulation blocks and roof tiles for building, for drainage aggregates, gaskets, seals and washers. If you've got a spare tyre, you can also recycle it yourself in a number of creative ways. For example:

 Bumper: If you live near a boatyard or marina, ask if anyone there would like to use it as a bumper.

 Swing: If you've got a big enough tree, make a tyre swing.

Flowerbed: Stack them on top of each other, fill them with soil and use them to grow potatoes. To harvest, pull the stack apart tyre by tyre and gather the spuds!

Green Products

Increasingly, manufacturers of cars and components are aware of green driving issues. It's now possible to buy environmentally friendly batteries – Varta Automotive also goes to considerable lengths to ensure that the development, production and ultimate disposal of its batteries are as green as possible. Meanwhile, Firestone has developed fuel-saving tyres for most types of car. However, until you need new ones, a few simple but effective measures will help you to extend the life of your existing tyres:

 Inflation: Make sure they are inflated to the correct pressure – check inflation levels on a weekly basis.

 Balanced: Make sure your tyres are correctly balanced and rotated regularly.

 Weight: Make sure your car isn't overloaded.

 Speed: Watch your speed, and brake and start gently to avoid skidding.

Clean Green Machine

If you think of your car as a tool and not as a status symbol, then washing it becomes less important than keeping it roadworthy and economical. Not washing your car also saves water. But there are times when it needs cleaning – the salt used to grit roads in winter is corrosive and needs washing off, and you should keep windscreens (front and rear), windows, lamps and licence/vehicle registration plates clean at all times.

Green Car Wash

There are lots of green ways to wash your car.

Cleaning Tips

☑ **Don't use a hosepipe if you can avoid it**: If you do use one, do so only for rinsing. Even then it should have a trigger nozzle to improve pressure and reduce water consumption.

☑ **Use an eco-detergent**: Or don't use a detergent at all. Non-eco detergents contain chemicals that encourage algae to grow, and if these get into local watercourses, algae bloom can be a real problem for other wildlife.

- **Wash your card in the shade**: Sunshine evaporates off the water so you'll need to use more! Wash it in the shade or on an overcast day.
- **Wash it less frequently**: Dust it off instead and wait for heavy rain!
- **Try an earth-friendly polish**: There are lots of green products on the market, which clean and polish without harming the environment.

Have You Thought Of?

Washing your car on the grass? This will give the lawn a drink and the soil will help break down any impurities in the water to prevent them from getting into storm ways, drains and local water courses.

Checklist

- **Walk**: Make short journeys on foot.
- **Get on your bike**: Make sure you wear a helmet and a high-visibility vest and have some good lights.
- **Take public transport**: Enjoy the savings and make the most of your time on the journey.
- **Consider a scooter**: Scooters offer good fuel economy, and reduced emissions make them a relatively green choice.
- **Share journeys**: Or join a car pool.
- **Consider the type of car you run**: Biofuel, LPG/Auto Gas, all-electric, hybrid.
- **Use green driving techniques**: To reduce fuel consumption and save the planet.
- **Tyres**: Be careful how and where you recycle your tyres.
- **Car wash**: Let the rain wash your car for you.

Getting
Away

Green Tourism

Increased awareness of the growing environmental damage caused by our day-to-day habits and the emergence of affordable mass travel and tourism have, ironically, resulted in many people rushing to see places that may soon disappear. Of course, in doing so they contribute further to the environmental impact. There are ways in which we can see the world without harming it, and ways we can minimize our environmental footprint at the same time.

Disappearing Destinations

The effects of climate change have left very few places in the world untouched; rising temperatures affect the growing seasons of woodlands and forests and leave them open to attack from pests and diseases, while melting glaciers and rising sea levels threaten to engulf low-lying lands and islands in Europe, the Indian Ocean and Asia. Some popular tourist destinations are amongst the threatened areas. For example, Venice has seen an increased number of serious floods, while the Great Barrier Reef is under threat from rising water temperatures, over-fishing and coastal land use, which have placed undue stress on

the corals and led to several mass bleaching events in the past 10 years. The annual snowfall level in the Alps is also in decline, with many glaciers also threatened; and the once-pristine wilderness of the Arctic is melting at a rate five times faster than anywhere else in the world.

Have You Thought Of?

Investing in a solar-powered battery charger? This will cut down on the number of batteries ending up in landfill sites and keep your phone, camera and MP3 player batteries topped up.

Should I Go?

Around five per cent of global CO_2 emissions are produced by tourism. The first thing a green tourist must consider is their mode of transport. According to TerraPass, a company specialising in carbon offsetting, a round-trip flight from Los Angeles to Sydney – around 15,000 miles (24,000 km) – uses over 1,000 litres (300 gallons) of fuel and produces nearly 3 tons (around 3 tonnes) of CO_2 per passenger. Also, since endangered destinations are increasingly popular, many of these sites are increasingly overcrowded and therefore get more damaged; rising demand for cruises to the Arctic means more ships, greater environmental impact and potential for accidents such as the sinking of the *Explorer* in November 2007.

On the Other Hand...

Tourism is vital to many communities across the world and, in some places, has stimulated the development of conservation initiatives or low-impact, sustainable tourism methods, by which visitors can both enjoy the land and be culturally enriched by their travels. In some instances, the visitor may feel that the experience gained from eco or responsible tourism offsets some of the CO_2 emissions made on the journey.

Wherever You Roam

Wherever you go and however you get there, it is important to take care of the environment and to continue to think green. Take your green ways of living on holiday. Show the same concerns for the environment, emissions, food production and ethical trade as you would at home.

Top Tips for Responsible Travel

- **Respect the local environment**: Dispose of your trash responsibly – take it home and recycle or compost it.

- **Watch your step**: Many ecosystems are so fragile that just walking across the greenery or touching the coral can cause lasting damage. Stay on marked paths when walking.

- **Respect local traditions and customs**: Familiarize yourself with the cultural norms and the laws of your destination before you travel. Dress and act appropriately and ask before you photograph people.

- **Respect human rights**: Exploitation in any form is at odds with ethical consumerism and eco-travel and tourism.

- **Bargaining or haggling may be expected**: But it should also reflect an understanding of a fair wage.

Staycation

A staycation is time spent by individuals and families relaxing at home, perhaps taking daytrips to visit attractions. They provide a viable green alternative to ordinary holidays. There are many benefits: they cost less than a vacation involving long or overseas travelling, and your spending money goes to local businesses, museums, galleries or places of interest. There is also less stress: no airport queues, flight delays, overweight or lost luggage, vaccinations or travel sickness, and you don't have to put pets in kennels or catteries.

How to Staycation

Having a break is very important, so if you decide to take a staycation make sure you think of it as a real vacation. Following some of these guidelines should ensure that you have a fun and relaxing time.

Staycation Guidelines

 Act as though you were going away: Do all the stuff you would do if you were going away. Pay bills in advance and tell people you will be away – put a message on your phone and e-mail to this effect.

Have You Thought Of?

Taking a refillable water bottle and a spare 'bag for life' on holiday? This will keep plastic waste from destroying the environment.

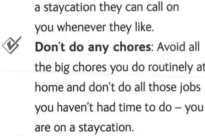 **Don't do any work**: Avoid at all times the temptation to do a bit of work or allow your employer to think that because you're on a staycation they can call on you whenever they like.

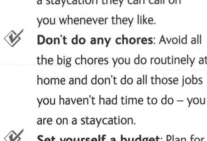 **Don't do any chores**: Avoid all the big chores you do routinely at home and don't do all those jobs you haven't had time to do – you are on a staycation.

Set yourself a budget: Plan for some lunches or dinners out, entry fees and souvenirs.

Plan fun things to do: Get some holiday brochures for your area and write a list of things to do, just as you would if you were in a strange place. If you went to Paris, you'd want to see the Louvre Museum; on a staycation, you'd take a look at the museums and galleries in your area.

Consider a green home swap: This is a staycation but in someone else's home while they stay in yours! Home swaps are increasingly popular, so look online for green schemes. You might swap your city flat for a rural cottage and know that the folks you've traded homes with are greenies like you.

Alternative Ways to Travel

As airfares have come down and disposable incomes have risen people have started flying more and more frequently, even though flying is the least eco-friendly mode of transport. There are plenty of alternative ways to travel and, although slower, they can be far more relaxing and enjoyable.

Flying

Per passenger mile, aeroplanes are roughly comparable to cars in fuel consumption, but while we are making efforts to drive less, air travel is one of the fastest-growing causes of air pollution and global warming. If you really must fly, then make sure you fly direct to your destination; think about taking one long trip instead of two or three short trips or weekend city breaks by air; and offset the carbon emissions of your flight.

Carbon Offsetting

Carbon offsetting is a way of cancelling out carbon emissions by investing in carbon-reducing initiatives such as reforestation and renewable energy. Carbon offsetting providers calculate how much carbon a certain activity, such as taking a flight, will have produced, and how much it will cost to offset. You can offset emissions for activities such as driving a car, using electricity and gas in your home and even eating meat. A search on the Internet will bring up many carbon-offsetting providers.

Reduce Your Carbon Footprint

Some environmental campaigners are concerned that carbon offsetting encourages people to continue burning fossil fuels and buy their way out of the problem, instead of changing their behaviour and reducing their carbon footprint. Don't fall into this trap – always consider whether a journey is necessary or whether there is an alternative form of transport.

Walking Holidays and Tours

Some of the most memorable travel moments can only be experienced on foot; in Venice it's the only way to get around, and in other cities or the countryside, walking is one the best, and the greenest, ways to get around. There is now a whole range of walking tours available: urban and rural, easy and difficult, and increasingly there are walking tours for people with disabilities, including wheelchair-accessible tours.

Is It for Me?

If you can walk at a relaxed pace for about two hours, then a walking tour might just be up your street but, like any outdoor activity, you need to be prepared for some unpredictable weather – and tired legs at the end of the day!

Tours on Offer

Many specialist tour operators offer walking holidays and will plan your vacation, provide a guide, carry your luggage between overnight stops and arrange meals. Some tours may be gentle, while others involve higher altitudes and slightly rougher terrain, so you need to know your physical limits. There are themed tours that take in cookery, painting or bird-watching, others include some horse- or bike-riding. There are walking tours for single travellers, families, women and people with disabilities. The more independent-minded may prefer to plan their own routes. Be aware that you'll need to map your journey in advance and book accommodation; travel light, as you'll be carrying your own stuff, perhaps including a tent and cooking equipment!

Benefits

If your are reasonably fit and like being in the open air, then there are many benefits to a walking tour:

Relaxed pace: It's the ultimate in slow travel.

 Healthy: You get fit and might even lose a bit of weight!

 No specialist gear is required: All you really need is a pair of sturdy boots or shoes.

Negligible environmental impact: Your impact on the environment is negligible.

Better by Bike

You don't have to be a professional cyclist or Yellow Jersey winner of the Tour de France to enjoy a holiday by bike. In many parts of the world, the bike is the primary mode of transport, so you won't be the only one on the road! There is now an enormous range of destinations and routes suited to every level of enthusiasm and fitness. Similarly, the types of bike tours range from the rough-and-ready to the luxurious. Travelling by bike is not only good for the environment, it's also good for your body – and the day's exercise will work up an appetite

for the local food. Like walking tours, many bike tours transport your luggage between overnight stops and many have support vehicles in case your bike, or legs, fail! Most also provide the bikes, so you don't need to take your own. Other self-guided bike tours are more suited to the independent traveller who wants to set their own pace; these often provide maps and suggested routes and can organize accommodation as well.

My Own Bike?

If you're planning your own itinerary, it's likely you'll want to take your own bike since it's comfortable and any quirks are familiar to you. Most airlines accept bikes – for a price. Generally the handlebars need to be fixed sideways and the pedals removed. Check your selected airline's rules and charges as they do vary considerably. The same goes for rail and ferry companies.

Let the Train Take the Strain

In environmental terms, train travel is fairly green. It is more energy-efficient per passenger mile than aeroplane or car travel, and the carbon emissions are less damaging to the environment than those from aeroplanes because they are not released directly into the upper atmosphere.

Benefits of Train Travel

Train travel is comparatively cheap and stress-free, and you are able to see the countries you're passing through. Think of the famous Orient-Express or the Trans-Siberian Express from Moscow to Beijing; or how about the California Zephyr from Chicago to San Francisco, or the Ethan Allen Express from New York to Vermont to enjoy the colours of a New England autumn? There are many other benefits of train travel:

- **Discounts**: Train companies offer a range of discounts to students, young people, senior citizens and families. In some countries, discounts are available to service personnel and other key workers, so check what's on offer.
- **No peak season**: Unlike aeroplanes, most railways don't have peak-season prices, although there may be premiums for travelling at peak times in the day.
- **Arrive at the heart of your destination**: One of the best things about travelling by train is that the stations, unlike airports, are usually right in the heart of the cities and towns they serve, so you're only a short bus or taxi ride away from your accommodation.
- **There's less hassle at check-in**: No need to arrive two hours early, no security checks – although on some cross-border journeys these may occur.
- **You can take liquids on board**: And your shampoo won't be confiscated!
- **You can stretch your legs at any time**: Not just when the seatbelt sign goes off.
- **Reclining seats**: Overnight travellers can upgrade to reclining seats or sleeping compartments. If you're willing to share with a same-sex stranger, the price is lower.
- **Entertain yourself**: You can use your laptop or MP3 player and many train services offer free Wi-Fi connection. If you prefer peace, some services have quiet carriages where mobile phone use is barred.

Coach Potatoes: Bus and Coach Travel

Although they still run largely on fossil fuels, buses and coaches are still a reasonably green method of travel. For short hops, or for intercity and inter-country journeys, they also offer a relatively cheap and efficient way of getting around.

All Over the World

You can cross North America, Canada and Australia in Greyhound Buses. In Australia, try the Oz Experience, which offers hop-on, hop-off bus tour passes for the adventurous backpacker. In the UK, travel by Megabus or National Express; National Express also has regular European routes, including destinations as exotic as Moscow and Marrakech. Visit any of, or all, 600 destinations in New Zealand with InterCity buses. The wonders of the Internet now mean that, whatever your intended destination, you can, with the click of a mouse, find bus and coach companies that serve that place. Remember that many companies offer discounts, so ask what's available.

Organized Tour

If you prefer, you could always travel on an organized coach tour of a particular country or region and have

your accommodation laid on each night. This is a great way to see particular places of interest such as monuments and museums, as the entry price is often included in the tour price and you get a knowledgeable local guide, too.

Tips for Bus and Coach Travel

Coach or bus travel is slower – buses and coaches are generally speed-limited to around 55 mph (88 km/h) – and if you've got very long legs, it can be uncomfortable. However, these tips should ensure a safe, comfortable journey:

Plan your route in advance: But be prepared for delays in transit.

 Take an inflatable neck pillow: Especially on night journeys.

Avoid seats located over the wheels: Especially if you suffer from travel sickness, as the vibrations here can aggravate the condition.

 Belt up: Most long-distance coaches have these and, in most instances, wearing a seat belt is the law.

Ship Ahoy: Ferries and Green Cruises

Fancy island-hopping around the Cyclades in the Aegean Ocean, seeing the Northern Lights in the Arctic Circle, visiting the Galapagos Islands or whale-watching? Then a green cruise might just be the thing.

Murky Past

In the recent past, the cruise industry has been guilty of paying too little attention to the environment. Major issues included waste dumping at sea, including the discharge of untreated sewage, oily bilge water and grey wastewater, and polluting emissions.

Clean Future

To its credit, the industry is making important changes to its practices. In 2003, the Cruise Lines International Association joined with Conservation International on a range of initiatives, which included drawing up a global map of cruise navigation maps that identified sensitive eco-areas.

Some cruise liners are installing recycling bins throughout their ships; have environmental officers and trainers as part of their crew; are supporting local green initiatives at their ports of call; and using organic and ethically traded produce on their menus and sustainable materials through their ships during refits. If you plan on cruising, check the cruise line's green credentials before you book.

Voluntourism

So far, all the discussions about green travel and vacation have been 'me' focussed – about the pleasures of vacationing and the value of experiencing new cultures and places. Perhaps it's time to give something back and volunteer your time, energy and skills to make the planet a better place. More than just a holiday, volunteering on an environmental, wildlife or humanitarian project can literally be a life–changing experience. Voluntourism offers a chance to work for as long as you wish, from a few days to several months, in fascinating places that need your help.

Who Can Do It?

Everyone can volunteer! Some organizations encourage families to work together and there's no upper age limit. You can participate in a project in almost any part of the world: repairing dry-stone walls in the Lake District or digging a well in an African village. You don't need to know the language either, as local project co-ordinators are there to help. They will often set up activities to do in your free time, so that you get to see more of the country you're working in.

Be Prepared

Before you sign up to any project, make sure you are prepared. You may need to:

- **Be open to another culture**: The beliefs, values and customs may be very different from your own.
- **Forego some modern conveniences**: Such as hot showers, flushing toilets, air conditioning etc.
- **Be patient, tolerant and willing to learn.**

The Costs

Volunteering doesn't mean there are no financial costs involved. You are usually liable for your own travel expenses, visas, insurance and pre-trip medical checks and vaccination costs. Also, regardless of whether the organizers of the project are charities or commercial concerns, they will charge a fee – which can be quite large. To cover costs, many volunteers arrange sponsorship or undertake fundraising activities before they travel.

Do Your Homework

If you want to volunteer your time and skills, then do your homework first:

- **Search the Internet**: www.transitionsabroad.com is a useful place to start as it has links to many organisations offering voluntourism.
- **Match your skills to the projects on offer**: If you like children, what about a school or orphanage? If you like nature, perhaps you should consider a conservation project?

☑ **Find out what your fee covers**: You should not pay for programme information and you should be able to check out alumni for verification.

☑ **Help the local community**: Choose a project that is run in conjunction with local people, and look for an organization that will return 90–100 per cent of the funds it receives directly to the projects it administers.

Don't Be Daunted

If this all sounds a bit daunting, check out ordinary tour and travel companies; some have special low-priced pre-season and post-season volunteer vacations on offer, such as beach clean-ups or campsite set-up, break-down and restore weeks. It's a way to start thinking about putting something back – and a great way of seeing the world at the same time.

Checklist

☑ **Stay at home**: Explore your local area instead of going overseas.

☑ **Offset your carbon emissions**: If you decide to fly.

☑ **Enjoy a walking or cycling holiday**: And get fit at the same time.

☑ **Travel by train**: And arrive in the centre of your destination.

☑ **Use the Internet**: Book a bus or coach anywhere in the world.

☑ **Volunteer**: Use your vacation to volunteer on an environmental, wildlife or humanitarian project.

Work

More Work, Less Energy

Doing an energy audit is a good way to see how your workplace can be greener, produce less waste and be more energy-efficient and cost-effective. A number of organizations, including Friends of the Earth, offer these types of energy audits. Some can be done online and many are completely free of charge, so it's well worth arranging one for your workplace. An energy audit will mean that not only is your workplace greener, but also that any changes being made are all within current legislation.

Temperature

If the temperature in your office rises by just 2° C, you'll create enough CO_2 in one year to fill a hot-air balloon! Turn down the heat by just 1° C and you'll feel more awake, have fewer headaches and feel less tired at the end of the day. Likewise, try turning off the air conditioning for one hour a day, perhaps one hour before the office closes. Better still, switch it off completely and open a window, if you can.

Let There Be Light

Good light is important to work by, but often offices have banks of ceiling lights that flood the entire room, even when there are only a few people working in it. Wherever possible, use a desk light instead, and position it to illuminate the space in which you are working. Position the lamp to one side (not behind you or you'll be working in your own shadow) and use the shade or reflector to shine the light downwards onto the work at hand. Fit lamps with energy-saving bulbs, and switch them off at the wall when not in use.

Light the Way with LEDs

LED (light-emitting diode) lamps are the next step forward in green lighting technology, so perhaps you can persuade your boss to invest in these for the office by stressing their green and long-term energy-efficient credentials. LED lights have been around for some time: they are the lights on your music system and the standby lights on your TV and DVD players. LEDs are illuminated by the movement of electrons, so they don't have a filament to burn (where much of the wasted energy comes from in ordinary light bulbs); consequently they generate very little heat. Unlike low-energy bulbs, LEDs don't contain any mercury, which can make the disposing of low-energy bulbs a problem. A further development is the OLED (the O stands for Organic): these are made of thin organic material layered between two electrodes that produce light when an electrical charge is applied. The thin layers mean that OLEDs can be very flexible in structure; they can even be woven into fabrics, which means that the office blinds and curtains could start providing low-cost, energy-efficient light!

Lights Out

Light pollution is a serious problem, especially in towns and cities. While it is important that the streets are well-lit for safety, many business and office buildings are unnecessarily ablaze with light at night despite the calls to save energy. Not only is this wasted energy, it also makes seeing the night sky near impossible, and it confuses birds such as nightingales and blackbirds, who now often sing throughout the night because of the light in cities.

Light and Energy Saving Tips

- **Signs**: Put up signs telling co-workers to switch off lights and appliances.
- **Use energy-saving bulbs**: These use less energy than regular light bulbs.
- **Make use of natural light and ventilation**: Open shades, blinds and windows where possible.
- **Turn lights off**: If you're out of a room for more than 15 minutes, turn the lights off. This rule also applies to portable heaters and cooling fans.
- **Don't over-light**: Light only where needed but make sure safety is not compromised.
- **Don't waste light**: Turn lights on only when needed; ask for sensors to be installed in lavatories so that lights are switched on and off when someone enters and leaves.
- **Turn out the lights at the end of the day.**

Please Leave a Message

Did you know that a telephone answering machine uses electricity 24 hours a day, seven days a week, and can consume up to 100 kW per year? Unplug it when you're in, and only plug it in when you leave the office.

Water Works

We spend a great deal of our lives at work, and it is vital that we take the green habits we practise at home to work with us. When we switch on the light at work, wash our hands or throw away a used envelope instead of reusing or recycling it, we are using up precious resources. Water is just one of those vital resources: it is in short supply, so make sure it isn't wasted.

Don't Be a Drip!

While it is acceptable not to pull for a pee at home, in shared lavatories in the workplace, it's a must! Nevertheless, old lavatory cisterns use a lot of water in the flush – more than is actually needed – so perhaps it's time the boss installed low- or dual-flush lavatories. If this isn't possible, then you could still fit hippo bags (often available free of charge from your water company) that fit in the cistern and reduce the amount of water used. Remember, too, that dripping taps waste an incredible amount of water – if there's one in your office lavatory, let the maintenance department know about it and ask for it to be fixed.

Hands Off

Another way to reduce the amount of water used at work is to encourage water-saving hand washing: don't run more water than is needed, or, better still, install push-button taps that dispense a measured amount of water. And while you're in the office washroom, are the hand-washing liquids eco-friendly and the paper towels recycled? If not, then get greening in the smallest room! If there's a dishwasher in the kitchen, make sure it's washing a full load and not just one cup.

Soft As A Baby's...

While we're on the subject, ask yourself whether you really need lavatory paper that is made out of virgin paper? The short answer is no! Ask your boss to switch to recycled paper – and make it single-ply! Better still, persuade the company to demonstrate deep-green credentials and opt for earth-friendly, unbleached, chlorine-free paper. Recycled paper needs to be pulped and de-inked before it can be made into new paper; many processing plants still use chlorine bleaches which can react with the paper fibres and create harmful toxic compounds such as dioxins.

Water-cooler Moments

The advantage of a water cooler is that it provides staff with nicely chilled water. That's it. Let's face it, 'water cooler moments' – those interesting discussions full of witty repartee – only really happen on TV. There are two types of cooler: ones fed by bottles and those that are mains-fed. With bottled-water coolers, there may be green issues around the source or provider (some bottled water is produced by big-name multinational companies), the transport costs and emissions, and the manufacture (and disposal) of the plastic bottles themselves. All water coolers need electricity to run them (another machine working 24/7), and some models also use UV light to kill any bacteria in the dispenser part of the machine. Mains-fed coolers provide chilled tap water, and there's probably a fridge or two in the building already doing this job! If some people baulk at the idea of drinking tap water, that's not a problem: get some filter jugs to fit in the fridge, or fit a filter to the tap (faucet).

Ditch the Disposables

If you do have a cooler, cut down on the waste paper or plastic from the cups by using just one – put a sticky label on it with your name on. Or bring in your own glass and encourage others to do the same. Don't fill the kettle with chilled water as it will require more power to heat it up. Keep a jug of filtered water at room temperature for tea- and coffee- making, and remember to put only as much water as you need in the kettle. Get rid of the Styrofoam cups and the throwaway cutlery; bring a mug, knife, fork and spoon to work and enjoy your lunch in green style. And while we're on the subject of food, why not have a waste bin in the kitchen area for tea bags and non-meat or dairy waste to go into a composter.

Computers

Once only used for specialist operations, computers are now on virtually every desk and in every home. They may have got smaller and more efficient, but they still need energy to power them – whether battery or mains electricity – and they need huge amounts of resources to manufacture and dispose of them.

On Standby

Did you realise that leaving your computer on standby still requires up to 30 per cent of the energy it needs when it's on? It may not be processing any information, but power is still being fed to the computer and all the peripherals (mouse, keyboard and printers).

Shut Down

Make sure you shut down and switch the computer off at the wall at night to avoid phantom power consumption (check first with your IT department to make sure that it doesn't need to be on for overnight back-up or system maintenance). While you're in a meeting or at lunch, you can save energy by enabling the power save/management options. In Windows this is found in Settings/Control Panel/Power Options; in Macs, go to System Preferences/Energy Save/Sleep. This will send your computer to sleep and save up to 70 per cent of the energy use; you can also set it to shut your computer down and switch off the screen if it isn't in use for a specified period, saving 100 per cent of the energy!

Re-install

It's not unusual for computers to get sluggish as time goes on; the updates, installations and applications running that you don't need all impact on their performance. This means that there's more wear on the hard drive and more electricity is used than is really needed. Try re-installing your software, and remove anything that you never use to free up space on the hard drive, and make your system perform faster and more efficiently.

Green Screens

When it comes to electricity, the computer screen or monitor is the biggest consumer, and the bigger the screen, the more power it uses.

Screen Energy Saving Tips

Have your screen only as bright as you need it: Really bright screens eat power.

Animated screen-savers consume electricity: Ditch the tropical island or cute basket of kittens screen saver and leave it blank instead.

Computer screen colours use electricity in different amounts: The colour white displayed on a CRT (Cathode Ray Tube) computer monitor uses 25 per cent more electricity than when black is displayed. Reading white text on a black background is hopeless after a time, so try a green background instead! It uses less power and is very restful on the eyes, too!

Recycle and E-cycle

When your workplace decides to upgrade its computers and get rid of its old machines, ask for them to be donated to a charity instead of going to a landfill site. Most machines that are thrown out simply look old, but they may work perfectly well. If they work, keep as many of the existing components such as keyboards and mice. If your company hands its machines to a recycling company, ask where, and how, the recycling will be done – some of the components in computers are toxic and need careful handling, but some companies ship old computers to the Far East where cheap labour is used to strip down machines to remove reusable metals.

The Paperless Office

The greenest paper is no paper at all. Unfortunately, the digital revolution did not deliver a completely paperless office, but there are ways that we can reduce the amount we use, and the amount we waste.

Types of Paper

Start by buying chlorine-free paper with a higher percentage of post-consumer recycled content. Wherever possible, use a lighter weight paper for internal paperwork, and keep the better-quality paper for external communications. Glossy paper is not only more expensive than matt, it's also more difficult to recycle.

Top Tips for Paper Saving

 Print on both sides of the paper: Or use the reverse of old documents and misprints for faxes and printing drafts. Make scrap-paper pads by cutting sheets to size and stapling them together.

 Send emails and don't print them out: Save them in folders and then transfer to a disk at the end of say, three months.

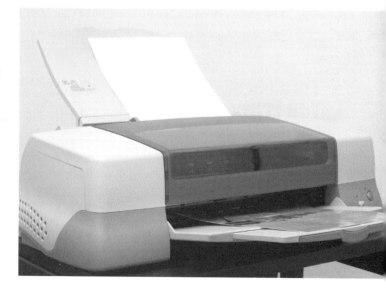

- **Check out new software like Greenprint**: It gets rid of blank pages from documents and can also convert to PDF for paperless document sharing.
- **Make the most of your computer**: Make folders and keep a tidy desktop. When one project or folder is complete, save it to disk and delete it from your desktop.
- **Decrease margins, footer and header sizes**: And don't use double line spacing for everyday print-outs.
- **When sending a fax**: Fax cover-sheet information can be incorporated into the first page of the document, or compose send-and-receive faxes via your computer.
- **Store letterheads electronically**: Rather than having paper stock printed. If you change location or phone number, you can alter it electronically
- **Reuse envelopes**: Especially for internal mail.
- **Print directly onto envelopes rather than sticky labels**: The sticky label makes the envelopes impossible to recycle into new paper. Buy envelopes without plastic windows as these are easier to recycle
- **Reuse paper files and folders**: Repair and re-label them.
- **Send seasonal e-cards**: To colleagues, suppliers and customers.
- **Keep the photocopier maintained**: Paper jams need removing carefully as shreds left behind just make more jams and waste paper.

Think Before You Print!

Make your computer do the work; most documents can be read or stored online, so don't print out unless it's absolutely necessary. If you really must print out e-mails, make sure you print on both sides of the paper. When you receive unwanted junk mail or printed catalogues at the office, ask the sender to remove you from their mailing lists before you send the offending item to the recycling bin.

Have You Thought Of?

Switching the copier off at night? Leave the copier on overnight and you will have wasted enough energy to make 30 cups of coffee.

Top Printer Tips

 Recycle toners and ink cartridges: And buy recycled or re-manufactured ones. Some companies will collect old cartridges when they deliver a new supply.

 You can easily refill your own cartridges: Do it when they're about 25 per cent full. Don't let them run totally dry, though. Every time you print without ink, it wears the print-head out.

 Unplug unused equipment: Printers and scanners that are only used occasionally should be unplugged.

 Avoid printing in colour wherever possible: Colour printing still uses black ink! And print in draft mode whenever you can.

Write On!

Paper may not have disappeared from the office but, somehow, pens always do! Look at the number of pens your workplace gets through and imagine where they all end up: in landfill sites. There's no need for this as pens can be recycled, so if you're in charge of the stationery cupboard, insist on pens and pencils made from recycled material. Make sure the pens are refillable, or why not treat yourself to a lovely fountain pen? Get it engraved with your name or initials: you'll be amazed at how you never lose it and how no-one picks it up in error.

Post-it Notes

Post-it notes are either too small or too big so you always end up using more than you need! Put up a whiteboard instead so messages can be left and then erased when read.

Commuting

The commute is the bane of many people's work day. All that pollution it creates puts pressure on the environment too. Have you considered the alternatives? Would your employer consider allowing you to telecommute? You could get fit by cycling to work, or enjoy a gossip with co-workers by joining a car pool.

Telecommuting

The digital revolution has not only made a difference to how we work but it has also opened up possibilities as to where we work. Thanks to instant messaging, e-mail, video-conferencing and VoIP (Voice over Internet Protocol), we now have the ability to telecommute (to work from home).

Savings

Telecommuting saves time, money and energy. Employees show that they are equally, if not more, efficient when they telecommute; it saves on the cost of travel and, for employers, on the cost of housing employees. And by not physically commuting, workers aren't adding to their carbon footprint.

Green Your Commute

If telecommuting is out of the question and you do have to travel to your workplace, walk, cycle or take public transport to work where possible. See the chapter Getting Around, pages 194–213, for more information.

Go to work by bike

Ask your employer to provide a secure place for bikes to encourage staff to go green. There are schemes by which employers can buy bikes at reduced costs and taxes on behalf of their employees.

Driving

If you do drive to work, why not form a car pool where rides can be shared or co-workers picked up and dropped off at central points (like railway and bus stations). If your business has a fleet of vehicles, see if any can be converted to LPG, or replaced with electric cars for short journeys around town. And if your employer is city-based, why not swap the car for a company scooter?

Green Work Environment

The key to greening any workplace successfully is to convince employers and staff of the benefits, both micro (the personal and immediate work environment level) and macro (the bigger, global level). It's the support of co-workers and employers that counts, but someone's got to start the ball rolling! Why not offer to be the green representative at your workplace so you can lead by example and encourage others to adopt green ways?

Ramp Up the Recycling

Make your workplace earth-friendly: set up some strategically placed paper recycling bins and suggest the document-shredder waste be used for wormeries or compost. Or offer it, and waste cardboard, to a local business as packaging material. You can do the same with polystyrene packaging material or even reuse any offending Styrofoam cups to make good drainage in plant pots, window boxes and troughs – you can use them to plant up some of the beneficial plants listed below to green your office.

Green Rules

Whether you work from home or in an office, there are three green rules that everyone should follow:

 Use what you already have: Don't buy more paper, gadgets or gizmos than you use or need.

 Use what others have discarded: Recycle office furniture, shelving and filing cabinets.

 Replace with the greenest you can get: When the time to buy does come round, make sure you buy the most energy-efficient items.

Bring in the Green

Certain plants have, according to NASA, been proven to be positively beneficial in the workplace. Constantly circulating oxygen and absorbing CO_2, plants are better (and more ecologically sound) than the synthetic pine or floral fragrances in air fresheners. Some of the plants proven to be effective filters for pollutants are:

- **Green Spider Plant** (*Chlorophytum elatum*).
- **Aloe vera**.
- **Bamboo Palm** (*Chamaedorea Seifrizii*).
- **Mother-in-law's-tongue** (*Sansevieria Laurentii*).
- **Peace Lily** (*Spathiphyllum*).

Checklist

- **Turn down the temperature**: You'll save energy and may feel more awake.
- **Don't waste light**: Good light at work is important, but turn lights off when they are not needed or being used.
- **Use recycled lavatory paper**: Ask your boss to make the switch.
- **Put your computer to sleep**: Save energy by not leaving it on standby.
- **Re-install your software**: Your computer will perform faster and more efficiently.
- **Don't waste paper**: Save emails and files on your computer, only printing when necessary.

Checklist

Included here are the checklists from the end of each chapter of the book. Use them to remind yourself of what to do. Tick them off as you go along!

Waste & Unwanted Goods

☐ **Think of the three Rs**: Reduce, reuse and recycle and make them part of you and your family's everyday routine.

☐ **Get a 'bag for life'**: Reduce the number of shopping bags you use.

☐ **Make the most of leftovers**: Reuse food for lunches or another meal.

☐ **Does your local area have a recycling service?**: If so, find out what they collect and make the most of it.

☐ **Find new homes for your unwanted belongings**: At garage sales, car boot sales or over the Internet.

☐ **Think about the source of items you buy**: Make a point of buying ethically and sustainably produced, recycled and recyclable goods wherever possible.

☐ **Investigate green bank accounts and investments**: Put your money where your mouth and your beliefs are.

Energy & Water

☐ **Calculate your carbon footprint**: Consider offsetting some or all of your carbon emissions.

☐ **Switch it off completely when not in use**: That means at the wall socket.

☐ **Don't leave electrical appliances on standby**: They're still using power.

☐ **Switch to energy-efficient light bulbs**: And turn the lights out when you leave a room empty – even low-energy bulbs still use energy.

☐ **Insulate and draught-proof your home**: This keeps the heat in and the cold out.

☐ **Turn your central heating down by just 1° C**: This will save money and energy.

☐ **Consider switching to a greener alternative**: Change energy tariffs, and give serious thought to wind or solar power.

☐ **Don't waste water**: It is a precious resource.

Cleaning

☐ **Handle with care**: Even though they are green, take care when handling all cleaning products; wear rubber gloves and wash your hands afterwards, too.

☐ **Spot test**: Do a spot test of your green cleaner on a hidden area before applying it to the entire surface.

☐ **Replace cleaning essentials with green alternatives**: In most homes, the cleaning *essentials* really consist of dish-washing liquid, laundry detergent, disinfectant, a scourer and bleach. Eco-friendly varieties of all of these are available.

☐ **Bicarbonate of soda**: This has many uses – it's a great deodorizer, a desiccant, a stain remover and a de-greaser.

☐ **Vinegar**: This is one of the best green cleaners. Use it for stain and odour removal, as a descaler, as an anti-bacterial cleaner and to get rid of mildew and mould.

☐ **Lemons and salt**: Lemons are acidic and anti-bacterial and the granular nature of salt makes it ideal as a scourer.

☐ **Use hydrogen peroxide, eucalyptus oil and borax**: These can all be used to clean the home in an environmentally friendly way.

☐ **Reuse and recycle**: Old T-shirts and tooth- and nailbrushes can be reused as cleaning implements.

Garden

☐ **Grow flowers**: Even if these are in a window box, hanging basket or container garden.

☐ **Grow food**: Choose from cabbages, carrots, peas, beans, lettuces, potatoes or fruit.

☐ **Choose organic fertilizers**: Synthetic fertilizers are cocktails of chemicals.

☐ **Get composting**: This will reduce your household waste and return nutrients to your garden.

☐ **Start a wormery**: Dispose of food waste even if you do not have a garden.

☐ **Practise organic weed control**: Use a green alternative to chemical weed controls or mulch around plants to prevent weed growth in the first place.

☐ **Deal with unwanted insects by companion planting**: Look on the Internet to find out which plants deter which insects.

☐ **Consider a living roof**: Create a haven for insects and improve the air quality in your town.

Food & Drink

- [ ] **Consider switching to organic, Fairtrade and ethically produced food**: There are many benefits for you and the environment.

- [ ] **Buy local, seasonal food**: It will be cheaper and won't have travelled across the world to your plate.

- [ ] **Can you afford free-range meat and poultry?**: It may be worth a little extra money to know that your dinner was raised humanely.

- [ ] **Avoid food waste**: Plan ahead, thinking about meals and portions, and your shopping bill may also be reduced.

- [ ] **Store your food correctly**: This will prolong its life and reduce food waste.

- [ ] **Try and cut down on food packaging waste**: How can you reduce, reuse and recycle your food packaging waste?

Fashion & Beauty

- [ ] **Be a conscious consumer**: Buy what you *need*, not what you want.

- [ ] **Buy ethically produced and organic goods**: Wherever possible.

- [ ] **Use the Internet**: Search out companies, products and suppliers who are actively working towards green principles.

- [ ] **Look after your wardrobe**: Carefully clean, iron and store your clothes.

- [ ] **Repair and reuse your existing wardrobe**: By mending or tailoring clothes.

- [ ] **Recycle clothes you never wear**: Consider donating to charity, swapping with friends or selling on eBay.

- [ ] **Look at natural beauty products**: And avoid the cocktail of chemicals that may have been tested on animals.

Celebrations

☐ **Remember the three Rs**: Reduce, reuse and recycle.

☐ **Buy local, organic and fair-trade**: Including food and presents.

☐ **Make a donation**: Donate to charities and aid organisations in lieu of personal gifts.

☐ **Cut down on waste**: By reusing paper and sending e-cards.

☐ **Donate your dress**: Consider donating your wedding dress to a charity.

☐ **Think about packaging**: Buy Easter eggs with the least amount of packaging or paint your own.

☐ **Don't buy an artificial Christmas tree**: Either decorate a houseplant or buy a tree from a local, sustainable source.

Getting Around

☐ **Walk**: Make short journeys on foot.

☐ **Get on your bike**: Make sure you wear a helmet and a high-visibility vest and have some good lights.

☐ **Take public transport**: Enjoy the savings and make the most of your time on the journey.

☐ **Consider a scooter**: Scooters offer good fuel economy, and reduced emissions make them a relatively green choice.

☐ **Share journeys**: Or join a car pool.

☐ **Consider the type of car you run**: Biofuel, LPG/Auto Gas, all-electric, hybrid.

☐ **Use green driving techniques**: To reduce fuel consumption and save the planet.

☐ **Tyres**: Be careful how and where you recycle your tyres.

☐ **Car wash**: Let the rain wash your car for you.

Getting Away

☐ **Stay at home**: Explore your local area instead of going overseas.

☐ **Offset your carbon emissions**: If you decide to fly.

☐ **Enjoy a walking or cycling holiday**: And get fit at the same time.

☐ **Travel by train**: And arrive in the centre of your destination.

☐ **Use the Internet**: Book a bus or coach anywhere in the world.

☐ **Volunteer**: Use your vacation to volunteer on an environmental, wildlife or humanitarian project.

Work

☐ **Turn down the temperature**: You'll save energy and may feel more awake.

☐ **Don't waste light**: Good light at work is important, but turn lights off when they are not needed or being used.

☐ **Use recycled lavatory paper**: Ask your boss to make the switch.

☐ **Put your computer to sleep**: Save energy by not leaving it on standby.

☐ **Re-install your software**: Your computer will perform faster and more efficiently.

☐ **Don't waste paper**: Save emails and files on your computer, only printing when necessary.

☐ **Green your commute**: Could you telecommute? Or get public transport or ride your bike to work?

☐ **Offer to be a green representative**: Lead by example and encourage others to adopt green ways in the workplace.

Further Reading

Anderson, W., *Green Up! An A-Z of Environmentally Friendly Home Improvements*, Green Books, 2007

Bongiorno, L., *Green, Greener, Greenest: A Practical Guide to Making Eco-Smart Choices a Part of Your Life*, Perigee Books, 2008

Bonnin, J. and McKay, K., *True Green Home*, National Geographic Society, 2009

Callard, S., *The Little Green Book of the Home*, Carlton Books Ltd, 2008

Callard, S. and Millis, D., *The Complete Book of Green Living: A Practical Guide to Eco-friendly Living*, Andre Deutsch Ltd, 2001

Costantino, M. and Steer, G., *Vinegar: 100s of Household Hints*, Star Fire Books, 2008

Corkhill, M., *Green Parenting: The Best for You, Your Children and the Environment*, Impact Publishing Ltd, 2007

Findley, M. and Formichelli, L., *The Complete Idiot's Guide to Green Cleaning*, Alpha Books, 2009

Gabriel, J., *The Green Beauty Guide*, HCI Books, 2008

Gow McDilda, D., *365 Ways to Live Green*, Adams Media, 2008

Grosvenor, M., *Green Living for Dummies*, John Wiley & Sons, 2007

Halpin, M. and Mason Hunter, L., *Green Clean: The Environmentally Sound Guide to Cleaning Your Home*, Andrews McMeel, 2005

Hegarty, M., *The Little Book of Living Green*, Nightingale Press, 2007

Hill, G. and O'Neil, M., *Ready, Set, Green: Eight Weeks to Modern Eco-Living*, Villard Books, 2008

Kostigen, T. and Rogers, E., *The Green Book*, Three Rivers Press, 2007

MacEachern, D., *Big Green Purse: Use Your Spending Power to Create a Cleaner, Greener World*, Avery Publishing Group Inc., 2008

Matheson, C., *Green Chic: Saving the Earth in Style*, Sourcebooks Inc., 2008

Reader's Digest, *The Green Home*, Reader's Digest, 2008

Schmidt, P., *The Complete Guide to The Green Home*, Creative Publishing International, 2008

Scott, N., *Reduce, Reuse, Recycle: An Easy Household Guide*, Green Books, 2004

Sivertsen, L. and T., *Generation Green*, Simon Pulse, 2008

Strauss, R., *Green Guides: Compost*, Flame Tree Publishing, 2009

Sutherland, D. and J., *Bicarbonate of Soda: 100s of Everyday Uses*, Star Fire Books, 2009

Trask, C., *It's Easy Being Green*, Gibbs M. Smith Inc, 2006

Websites

www.carbonfootprint.com
Calculate your carbon footprint on this website.

www.carpoolconnect.com
Search to find a carpool matching your commute.
Discuss carpooling and other related issues.

www.computeraid.org
The world's largest non-profit supplier of computers
to developing countries.

www.coopamerica.org
Organization that aims to harness economic power –
the strength of consumers, investors, businesses,
and the marketplace – to create a socially just and
environmentally sustainable society.

www.ebay.com
Buy and sell unwanted goods to prevent them
from going to landfill.

www.energysavingsecrets.co.uk
Over 100 articles written by experts about saving energy.

www.ethicalfashionforum.com
Trade association for the fashion industry, led by
businesses, for businesses, focused on social and
environmental sustainability.

www.freecycle.org
Keep stuff out of the landfill by giving and getting
items for free.

www.greenlivingtips.com
Green living tips for every part of your life.
You can sign up for a free newsletter.

www.greensceneusa.com
Articles and links on living green.

www.localfoodadvisor.com
UK site that helps you find the best local food producers,
suppliers, farmers' markets and restaurants in your area,

www.lovefoodhatewaste.com
Tips and recipes to reduce food waste.

www.recyclenow.com
Complete guide to recycling in the UK, including
what you can recycle and where to recycle near you.

www.reducereuserecycle.co.uk
UK guide to what and where you can recycle, green
shopping and transport, environmental organisations
and articles on living green.

www.slowfood.com
Organization founded to counteract the
disappearance of local food traditions and people's
dwindling interest in the food they eat, where it
comes from, how it tastes and how our food
choices affect the rest of the world.

www.transitionsabroad.com
A useful and comprehensive resource for working
abroad, studying abroad and cultural travel overseas.

www.usrecycleink.com
US site that pays cash for used cell phones,
empty printer cartridges and surplus printer
supplies. Also promotes responsible recycling
programs throughout schools, non-profit
organizations and corporate America.

Index